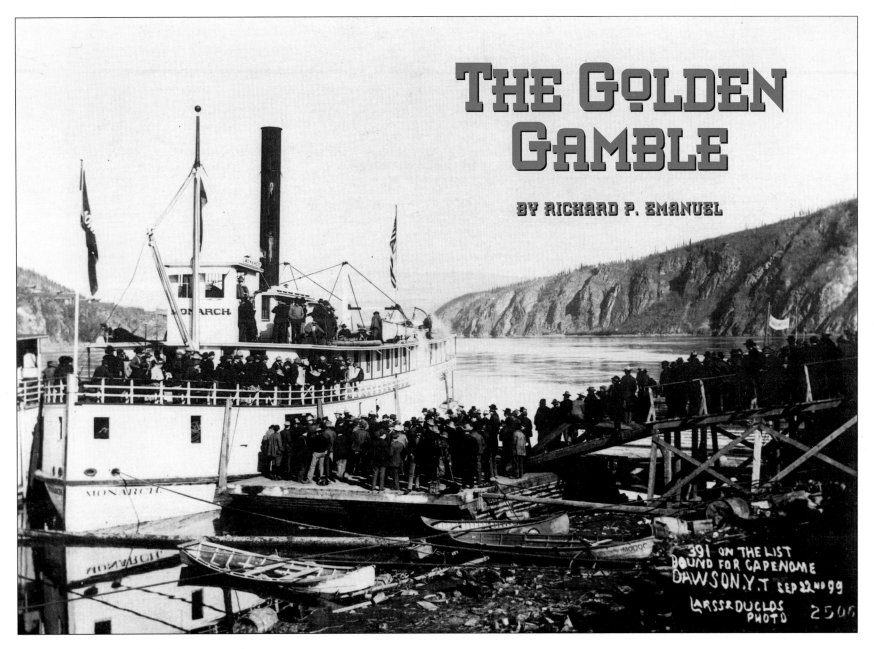

THE GOLDEN GAMBLE

BY RICHARD P. EMANUEL

To teach many more to better know and more wisely use our natural resources...

EDITOR
Penny Rennick

PRODUCTION DIRECTOR
Kathy Doogan

MARKETING MANAGER
Pattey Parker Mancini

CIRCULATION/DATABASE MANAGER
Linda Flowers

EDITORIAL ASSISTANT
Kerre Martineau

BOARD OF DIRECTORS
Richard Carlson
Kathy Doogan
Penny Rennick

Robert A. Henning, **PRESIDENT EMERITUS**

POSTMASTER: Send address changes to:
ALASKA GEOGRAPHIC®
P.O. Box 93370, Anchorage, Alaska 99509-3370

PRINTED IN U.S.A.

ISBN: 1-56661-035-4

Price to non-members this issue: $19.95

ALASKA GEOGRAPHIC® (ISSN 0361-1353) is published quarterly by The Alaska Geographic Society, 639 West International Airport Rd., Unit 38, Anchorage, AK 99518. Periodicals postage paid at Anchorage, Alaska, and additional mailing offices. Copyright © 1997 by The Alaska Geographic Society. All rights reserved. Registered trademark: Alaska Geographic, ISSN 0361-1353; Key title Alaska Geographic.

THE ALASKA GEOGRAPHIC SOCIETY is a non-profit, educational organization dedicated to improving geographic understanding of Alaska and the North, putting geography back in the classroom and exploring new methods of teaching and learning.

MEMBERS RECEIVE *ALASKA GEOGRAPHIC*®, a high-quality, colorful quarterly that devotes each issue to monographic, in-depth coverage of a northern region or resource-oriented subject. Back issues are also available. For current membership rates, or to order or request a free catalog of back issues, contact: The Alaska Geographic Society, P.O. Box 93370, Anchorage, AK 99509-3370; phone (907) 562-0164, fax (907) 562-0479, e-mail: akgeo@aol.com.

SUBMITTING PHOTOGRAPHS: Those interested in submitting photographs should write for a list of future topics or other specific photo needs and a copy of our editorial guidelines. We cannot be responsible for unsolicited submissions. Submissions not accompanied by sufficient postage for return by certified mail will be returned by regular mail.

CHANGE OF ADDRESS: The post office does not automatically forward *ALASKA GEOGRAPHIC*® when you move. To ensure continuous service, please notify us at least six weeks before moving. Send your new address and membership number or a mailing label from a recent *ALASKA GEOGRAPHIC*® to: Alaska Geographic Society, Box 93370, Anchorage, AK 99509. If your book is returned to us by the post office because of an incorrect address, we will contact you to ask if you wish to receive a replacement book for $5 (this covers postage costs only).

COLOR SEPARATIONS: Graphic Chromatics
PRINTING: Hart Press

The Library of Congress has cataloged this serial publication as follows:

Alaska Geographic. v.1-
[Anchorage, Alaska Geographic Society] 1972-
v. ill. (part col.). 23 x 31 cm.
Quarterly
Official publication of The Alaska Geographic Society.
Key title: Alaska geographic, ISSN 0361-1353.

1. Alaska—Description and travel—1959-
—Periodicals. I. Alaska Geographic Society.

F901.A266   917.98'04'505   72-92087

Library of Congress 75[79112] MARC-S.

COVER: *Capt. Elias Johnston, shown holding flakes and a cone of gold from one cleanup at his Cooper Gulch claim, prospered from the Klondike and Nome rushes. (Courtesy of Robert E. King)*

PREVIOUS PAGE: *Gold-seekers line up at Dawson to board the* Monarch *for Nome, Sept. 22, 1899. (Alaska State Library)*

FACING PAGE: *$125,000 in gold bricks is on display at the Assay Office of the American Bank of Alaska in Iditarod. (Courtesy of Pat Roppel)*

ABOUT THIS ISSUE: Richard P. Emanuel, free-lance writer and Anchorage resident, wrote the text for *The Golden Gamble*. The author and *ALASKA GEOGRAPHIC*® staff thank Frank B. Norris, historian with the National Park Service in Anchorage, for encouragement and advice in the initial stages of research for this issue, and especially for his generous review of the manuscript. Marc Blackburn, historian with the Seattle unit of the Klondike Gold Rush National Historical Park, also reviewed the manuscript and provided valuable material and invaluable aid. Several librarians and historical photo researchers helped find photos to complement the manuscript, including Candy Waugaman, a private collector from Fairbanks and Pat Roppel, historian and private collector from Wrangell; Ron Inouye, bibliographer at the Rasmuson Library, University of Alaska Fairbanks; Bruce Merrell and Dan Fleming with the Z.J. Loussac Library in Anchorage; Mina Jacobs with the Anchorage Museum; India Spartz with Alaska State Library in Juneau; Carolyn J. Marr, a photo researcher from Seattle; and the staffs of the Special Collections Division, University of Washington Libraries; the Oregon Historical Society; the California Historical Society; the Western Jewish History Center and the National Archives of Canada. ■

CONTENTS

Links of Gold 4

Outfitting the Rush:
   "Ho! For the Klondike" 12

Fever in the North 38

Legacy of Gold 76

From Gold Fields to Poor House 86

Bibliography 93

Index 94

LINKS OF GOLD

Gold is the seventy-ninth entry in the periodic chart of chemical elements. A soft and malleable metal in its native form, gold has nonetheless shaped human history.

In 1896, gold was found on the Klondike River, in Canada's Yukon Territory. The discovery was made in August but only whispers of the strike escaped the isolated region before the subarctic winter cut it off from the outside world. When demonstrable proof of the find landed in Seattle and San Francisco the following year in the form of tons of gold, it excited a stampede toward the dimly known North.

Most Klondike gold-seekers attempted routes that led through Alaska. They assailed Alaska mountains and navigated hazardous rivers in their rush toward the gold fields. Some called themselves argonauts, as had the California "Forty-Niners," after Jason and his companions of Greek mythology who sought the Golden Fleece. An estimated 100,000 gold-seekers set out to claim their fortunes in the Klondike.

Some 40,000 people made it to the boomtown of Dawson, at the confluence of the Klondike and Yukon rivers, although half of them arrived too late even to look for gold. About 4,000 miners, mostly those first on the scene, found gold along the Klondike and its tributaries. Perhaps 300 of these truly "struck it rich."

Most of the miners who found wealth quickly squandered their fortunes. Among the mass of humanity that surged northward toward glittering visions of gold, perhaps only 50 people wrested lasting wealth from the frozen and freezing gravels of the Klondike.

Once the staking of claims was complete throughout the Klondike district, the furor for gold passed to the west. Within five years, strikes on the beaches of Nome, in the Tanana Valley and elsewhere had scattered gold-seekers widely across Alaska. More localized stampedes continued to flare for another dozen years. The tumult slowly

FACING PAGE: *Well-wishers and dreamers crowd the docks along Elliott Bay on June 25, 1897, as the* Mexico *departs Seattle on its last trip north. (Courtesy of Pat Roppel)*

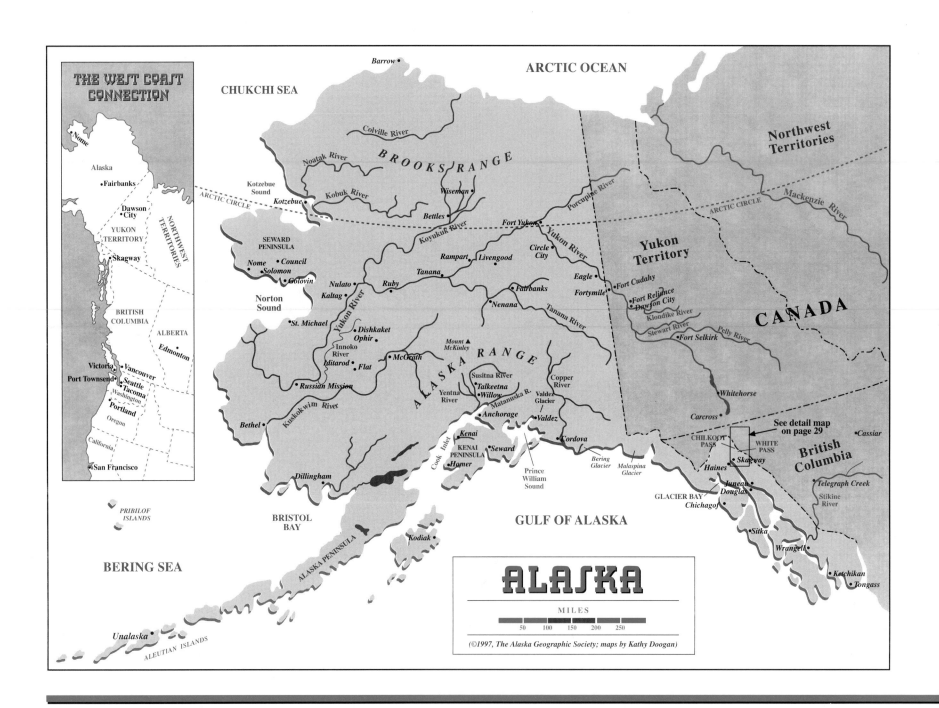

THE WEST COAST CONNECTION

Nome
Alaska
Fairbanks
Dawson City
YUKON TERRITORY
NORTHWEST TERRITORIES
Skagway
BRITISH COLUMBIA
ALBERTA
Edmonton
Victoria · Vancouver
Port Townsend · Seattle · Tacoma
Washington
Portland
Oregon
California
San Francisco

ARCTIC OCEAN

CHUKCHI SEA

Barrow

Colville River

BROOKS RANGE

Noatak River

Northwest Territories

Kotzebue Sound

ARCTIC CIRCLE

Kobuk River

Wiseman

Porcupine River

ARCTIC CIRCLE

Mackenzie River

Kotzebue

Bettles

Fort Yukon

Koyukuk River

Yukon River

Yukon Territory

SEWARD PENINSULA

Rampart Livengood

Circle City

Eagle

Fort Cudahy

CANADA

Nome · Council
Solomon
Golovin

Tanana

Fortymile

Fort Reliance
Dawson City

Nulato Ruby

Fairbanks

Klondike River

Norton Sound

Kaltag

Nenana

Tanana River

Stewart River

Fort Selkirk

Pelly River

St. Michael

Dishkaket
Ophir

Mount McKinley ▲

ALASKA RANGE

Innoko River

McGrath

Whitehorse

Iditarod Flat

Susitna River

Copper River

Russian Mission

Talkeetna
Willow

Carcross

Yentna River

Matanuska R.

Valdez Glacier

See detail map on page 29

Bethel

Kuskokwim River

Anchorage

Valdez

CHILKOOT PASS

WHITE PASS

Cassiar

Cordova

British Columbia

Kenai

Seward

Bering Glacier

Malaspina Glacier

Haines

Skagway

KENAI PENINSULA
Homer

Prince William Sound

GLACIER BAY

Juneau
Douglas

Telegraph Creek

Dillingham

Chichagof

Stikine River

PRIBILOF ISLANDS

BRISTOL BAY

GULF OF ALASKA

Sitka

Wrangell

Kodiak

BERING SEA

ALASKA PENINSULA

ALASKA

MILES
50 100 150 200 250

Ketchikan
Tongass

Unalaska

ALEUTIAN ISLANDS

(©1997, The Alaska Geographic Society; maps by Kathy Doogan)

RIGHT: *The 50-foot* Yukon *was the first sternwheeler on the Yukon River. It arrived on the river in 1869 and was the only steamer on the waterway throughout most of the 1870s. The first vessel to bear the name was crushed in the ice near Fort Yukon. Subsequent incarnations of the* Yukon *continued to cruise the river for decades. (Photo B93.5.15, Anchorage Museum)*

LOWER RIGHT: *A flurry of activity surrounds piles of supplies on the beach at Nome in 1900. (Photo by Lydia Mae Kellogg, courtesy of Steve McCutcheon)*

subsided, but it left behind an altered Alaska landscape.

Before the Klondike, for the first three decades after the United States had acquired Alaska from Russia, the American government had all but ignored its far-flung holding. Former Territorial Governor Ernest Gruening, in his book *The State of Alaska* (1968), labeled the period after Alaska's purchase "The Era of Total Neglect (1867-1884)." The succeeding period, 1884-1898, Gruening tagged "The Era of Flagrant Neglect."

Gruening had a point. Prior to 1884, Alaska was a customs and military district. It was governed by revenue cutters and by Army and Naval authorities whose only real presence was in the southeastern Panhandle. In 1884, the First Organic Act declared Alaska "a civil and judicial district." Civil authorities, all appointees, were a governor, district attorney, district judge, clerk and marshal, all based in the capital at Sitka. There were also four lesser-court judges and four deputies, stationed in Sitka, Wrangell, Juneau and Unalaska.

The legal code these 13 officials were to enforce was, oddly enough, the transplanted general legal code of the state of Oregon. Parts of the code ill-fit the northern, mostly maritime district. The mismatch scarcely mattered,

however, as the handful of authorities lacked funds for travel in their sprawling district, nor even to keep the courts in session.

The census of 1890 found 32,052 people in Alaska, the majority of whom were Natives. Yet there was not a single government hospital, no provision for the insane and no prison. In the entire, far-flung district there was only one wagon road more than two miles long, according to Gruening, and that had been privately built. The only things in Alaska that seemed to command federal interest were fur seals and salmon. Those marine resources had contributed perhaps $100 million to the national economy by the time of the Klondike strike, but well before the strike, both fur seals and salmon were in decline due to over-harvesting.

Homesteading was not legally recognized in Alaska: Individual ownership of land was not permitted outside of town sites. Nor had town sites been permitted until 1891. Thereafter, land within a town site could be surveyed and private lots sold, but there was no authority to establish a municipal government nor to levy taxes to support public purposes. Outside of town sites, only commercial interests could own land, a right exercised chiefly by trading posts and salmon canneries.

Lacking private real estate as security, no banks or insurance companies were willing to do business in Alaska. Thirty years of federal inaction and disregard had produced a legal vacuum and lack of capital that stymied those who sought to develop homes and businesses in the district.

A growing frustration with Washington, D.C., became the central theme in Alaska politics. Bills addressing Alaska problems had been introduced in Congress from time to time. Many had been acted upon in committee only to die unresolved as successive Congressional terms expired.

Copyright 1894.
By A.H. Waite.

Allen Gustison poses at Ballard, Wash. on May 1, 1898 in the latest northern outfit. (Photo B89.24.09, Anchorage Museum)

spurred the growth of Juneau into a town of 2,000.

The impact of the gold finds near Juneau was nothing compared with the Klondike and subsequent strikes in Alaska. The number of people who set out for the Klondike was three times the population of Alaska. Signs of Klondike fever appeared everywhere:

• Overnight, steamship lines that connected Alaska with West Coast ports feverishly expanded sailings and added ships.

• San Francisco, Seattle, Portland, Vancouver and other cities vied to outfit the argonauts. Guided by an aggressive and skilled public relations artist named Erastus Brainerd, Seattle won the battle, and with it, lasting economic spoils.

• Settlements already existing along the several trails to the gold fields exploded in size while new settlements burst into being.

• Transportation developed rapidly within Alaska, too, as men poured through mountain passes and onto its rivers. Trails were blazed and expanded, while along the Yukon River boat traffic grew. The White Pass and Yukon Railway, connecting the port of Skagway, Alaska, with Whitehorse on the upper Yukon River in Canada, gave convenient access to Yukon Territory and from there to interior Alaska for the first time.

• After years of neglect, U.S. government programs were launched to map, explore and evaluate Alaska's resources. Army camps were established and linked by telegraph. U.S. Geological Survey parties mapped topography and geology, sometimes in direct support of miners, at other times as pure exploration. Mail routes

Then came gold.

In the 1880s, prospectors sought and found gold in southeastern Alaska, having drifted north from gold fields in California and British Columbia. The Treadwell Mine on Douglas Island operated the largest gold mill in the world in the 1890s. It and other mines were broadly expanded, law enforcement and court proceedings were stepped up. And by fitful degrees, the federal government began to extend self-determination to Alaskans.

Between 1890 and 1900, the population of Alaska nearly doubled. Census figures in 1900 showed 63,592 Alaskans; most of the newcomers were non-Natives. By the end of the gold rush era, the percentage of Natives within Alaska's population had decreased substantially.

The rush for gold brought profound changes to Alaska, but it did not usher in a golden age. The land was too vast and too rugged to be tamed so quickly. And for all the furor, the quantity of gold produced was not overwhelming. Yet the effects of the rush were decisive. Alaska had been discovered anew.

Author Jack London, himself a Klondike veteran, wrote that the argonauts may have spent 10 times more wealth in seeking gold than the value of all the gold they found. Outfitters, steamship companies, riverboat operators, freighters, restaurateurs and grocers, hotel and roadhouse operators, bar owners and barkeeps all reaped a share of the golden economy.

Thousands of miners and entrepreneurs remained to settle Alaska. Others took their wealth and built on it in Seattle, San Francisco or elsewhere. Most gold-seekers returned to their loved ones with little more than stories to share.

But what stories! Those who had braved the Chilkoot Pass, Valdez Glacier or even the Yukon River were changed by their journeys. Tales of the Klondike or the golden beaches of Nome fired the imaginations and spirits of millions who had missed the rush. At least 300 gold-seekers published memoirs, and writers like London, Rex Beach and Robert Service captured for all time the flavor of the last great gold rush. Its mystique is alive today. ■

Josephine Patricia McDermott Nordhoff (1871-1920) and her husband, Edward, parlayed $1,200 into a thriving mercantile business thanks in large measure to the marketing frenzy that swept Seattle during the gold rush. (Photo 18095, Museum of History and Industry)

OUTFITTING THE RUSH:
"HO! FOR THE KLONDIKE!"

At 3 o'clock this morning the steamer Portland *from St. Michael for Seattle, passed up the Sound with more than a ton of solid gold aboard...*
— Seattle *Post-Intelligencer*,
July 17, 1897

Klondike Discovery

The stampede for Klondike gold began on July 17, 1897. On that day a steamship from St. Michael, on the Bering Sea north of the Yukon delta, docked in Seattle bearing a cargo of gold and garrulous prospectors. The great event came 11 months to the day after the first claim was staked on Bonanza Creek, the gold-rich discovery tributary of the Klondike River.

The official discoverer of Klondike gold was George Washington Carmack. The California-born son of a "Forty-Niner," Carmack had drifted north and married a Tagish Indian chief's daughter. On Aug. 16, 1896, he was prospecting in his usual desultory fashion with a pair of Tagish friends, Skookum Jim Mason, who was also Carmack's brother-in-law, and Mason's brother, Dawson (Tagish) Charley.

Just who first spotted gold on Rabbit Creek, as Bonanza was then called, is a matter of some dispute. Carmack claimed it was he, but Skookum Jim insisted that Carmack had been asleep under a birch tree when Jim, having just shot a moose, was cleaning a dish-pan in the creek and came up with gold.

Either way, the find was rich: a quarter-ounce of gold in each pan, worth about $4. At the time, 10 cents a pan was considered a good find. After a dance of celebration, the trio quickly panned out enough gold to fill an empty shotgun cartridge. The next morning, they staked four

FACING PAGE: *There was no end to the schemes and gadgets designed to relieve gold-seekers of their cash. "Just The Thing For Alaska" proclaims this sign for Portable Aluminum Houses advertised on Railroad Avenue in Seattle in 1898. (Photo 2500, Museum of History and Industry)*

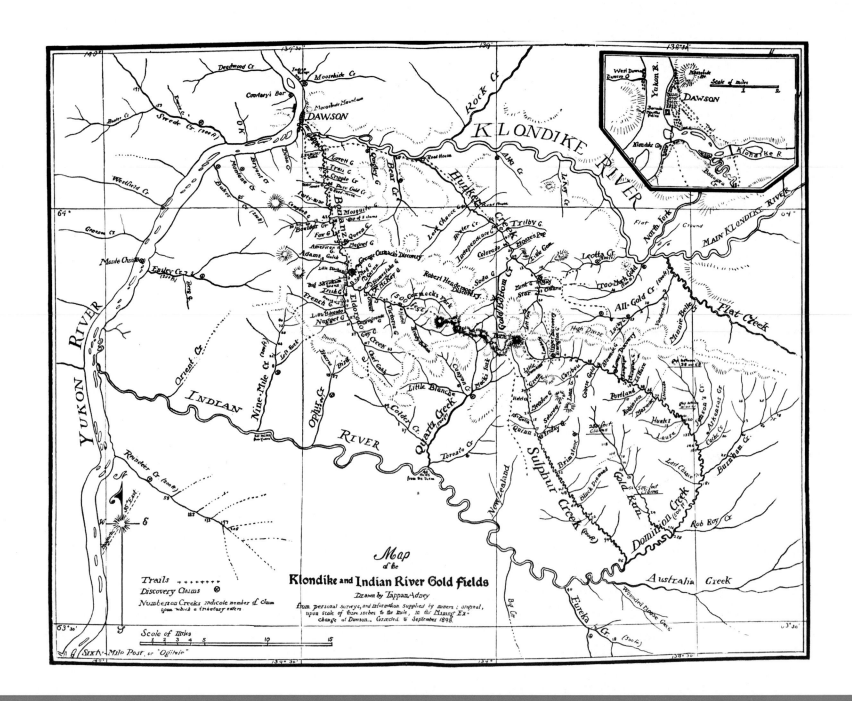

Map
of the
Klondike and Indian River Gold fields
Drawn by Tappan Adney

Camack

claims, each running along 500 feet of Bonanza Creek. Leaving Skookum Jim to guard their find, Carmack and Tagish Charley set off to register their claims at Fortymile, some 50 miles down the Yukon River.

Fortymile mining camp was a remote collection of cabins occupied by an assortment of eccentric sourdoughs. It had sprung up after the discovery of gold on a tributary of the Fortymile River, during the winter of 1886-87. It was late afternoon when Carmack and Charley nosed their log raft ashore in Fortymile. The camp was teeming with area miners who had come for supplies before winter closed in. Carmack relished breaking the news of his strike and did so with a dramatic flair in a crowded saloon, but many present were skeptical.

Carmack was an easygoing optimist who was known to stretch the truth. Some knew him as "Lying George." Still, there was Tagish Charley. And there was the shotgun shell full of gold. One by one, miners slipped away, slid their boats into the river and started upstream. By morning, Fortymile was all but deserted.

Word of the strike spread from sourdough to sourdough across the upper Yukon Valley, and by the end of August, Bonanza Creek was fully staked. Even richer ground had been found on a Bonanza tributary dubbed Eldorado Creek.

One enterprising man saw another method of mining gold. Joe Ladue rushed to Fortymile to register a town site where the Klondike empties into the Yukon River. He

The rush to the Klondike started with discovery of gold in the Bonanza Creek drainage. The discovery claim appears near the left edge of the photo in this view of the area in August 1898, two years after the initial find. (Photo by Tappan Adney, reprinted from The Klondike Stampede of 1897-1898 *[1900])*

named his town Dawson City, after George M. Dawson, a Canadian Geological Survey scientist who had explored and surveyed along the Alaska-Canada boundary.

As fall turned into bitter winter, prospectors through-out the region abandoned the modest claims they were working and rushed to the Klondike. By January 1897, there were only five wooden buildings in Dawson but it had 500 inhabitants, most all of them surviving in tents. Six months later, there were 5,000 people in town and the boom was just beginning. Within two years, lots on Dawson's main street sold for as much as $5,000 a frontage foot. The entrepreneurial Ladue, dubbed the mayor of Dawson City, had built and mined his own El Dorado.

Most of the early Klondike miners scraped up an abundance of gold that first winter, but word of their fortune did not spread beyond the Yukon Valley. In June, the Alaska Commercial Co.'s (ACC) sternwheeler *Alice* pulled into Dawson. It was soon followed by the *Portus B. Weare*, operated by the Seattle-based North American Trading and Transportation Co. (NAT&T), the ACC's upstart rival. The riverboats delivered food and liquor to Dawson and their arrival ignited a wild celebration. On the day the *Weare* departed, according to Klondike authority Pierre Berton, one Dawson saloon took in 400 ounces of gold.

When the *Alice* and *Weare* pulled into the current and started the long journey to St. Michael, they bore between them some 80 passengers. Also aboard were canvas bags and suitcases packed with gold. There were medicine

A venerable lady of the Yukon, the Alice *transported prospectors, miners, traders, tourists and tycoons along the river. On Sept. 6, 1896, the* Alice *carried word from William Ogilvie, a Canadian government surveyor then at Fortymile, to his superiors in Ottawa of a gold strike the previous month on Rabbit Creek, a tributary of the Klondike River. While awaiting instructions from his superiors, Ogilvie had spent the summer of 1896 at Fortymile and thus was one of the few government officials on hand when George Carmack registered his soon-to-be-famous claims at Fort Cudahy, across the Fortymile River from the settlement. The* Alice *continued to travel the river until 1953 when it was sold to the mission at Holy Cross. (Photo B67.32.4, Anchorage Museum)*

bottles, cans and jars jammed with gold. There was gold wrapped in blankets, so heavy that two men were needed to muscle them up the gangway. The decks of the *Weare* had to be propped with heavy timbers to support their load. The two boats puffed and chugged down the Yukon bearing together as much as three tons of yellow dust and nuggets.

Some miners heading downriver had sold their claims to late-comers at exorbitant prices. They were bound for civilization and did not plan to return. Others meant to spend money lavishly and then come back for more.

In St. Michael, the old Russian trading post on Norton Sound, the rowdy rich were ferried by Natives in kayaks and boats out to two battered ocean-going steamships. The ACC's *Excelsior* was headed for San Francisco while the NAT&T's *Portland* was Seattle-bound.

The *Excelsior* made landfall first, arriving in San Francisco on July 14. Those milling about the dock watched with astonishment as the scruffy miners disembarked burdened with treasure.

Tom and Salome Lippy wrestled a 200-pound suitcase onto the dock. Their personal fortune aboard the *Excelsior* amounted to some $85,000. Tom had been secretary of the Seattle YMCA in the spring of 1896 when a prescient hunch had sent him north with his wife. He had first staked a claim high on Eldorado Creek but later moved down to re-stake an abandoned claim to accommodate Salome. She wanted to live in a cabin and the timber was better at lower elevation. Turned out the gold was better, too. Eldorado Sixteen, the Lippys' claim, was the richest on the creek, eventually producing more than $1.5 million for the couple.

Sensational stories of the *Excelsior* and her passengers swirled around the streets of San Francisco. One sourdough had been seen toting a 30-pound poke into restaurants, where he ordered poached eggs nine at a time and left gold nuggets as tips. The Klondike rich were besieged wherever they appeared in San Francisco and the Lippys were effectively imprisoned in their Palace Hotel

Among 86 trading posts established along the coast of the "Westward," the common name for Alaska north of Sitka in the years immediately following U.S. purchase of Russian America, was St. Michael, established in 1833 by Lts. Michael D. Tebenkov and Adolph K. Etholin. As Russian trade along the river flourished, so did St. Michael. With U.S. purchase in 1867, the Alaska Commercial Co. took over the post. Agents stationed here, including Francois Mercier, hired Jack McQuesten, Arthur Harper, Al Mayo and others to manage their supply lines and posts along the Yukon. These early efforts forged a foundation that would grubstake the prospectors at the forefront of the gold rush. This earliest-known photo of St. Michael shows the log buildings, sod roofs and stockade of the Russian post. (Bancroft Library, Scammon Collection)

A hodgepodge of boats gathers at St. Michael. Located on an island about 60 miles north of the mouth of the Yukon River, St. Michael was the crossroads for river traffic and the ocean-going steamships that plied the Bering Sea and Pacific Ocean. (Photo PCA 245-19, Alaska State Library)

suite. Local newspapers spread tales of fabulous wealth and versions of those tales were wired across the nation.

The Battle for Gold Rush Trade

Excitement at the discovery of gold in the frozen North was palpable throughout the nation, but Seattle was pitched into a positive frenzy. Word spread that a second treasure ship was nearing, laden with even more gold.

When the vessel was still a day out, the Seattle *Post-Intelligencer* chartered a tugboat to intercept her. The tug *Sea Lion* met the *Portland* off Port Angeles in the early morning hours of July 17. A correspondent clambered onto the incoming ship and "was aboard long enough to get the thrilling story," the *P-I* soon reported. The vessels parted before dawn and the *Sea Lion* raced to Port Townsend, where a telegraph operator was roused and the story was filed.

There were about 2 tons of 80-percent-pure gold aboard the *Portland*, worth just under $1 million. The *Post-Intelligencer* portrayed the cargo conservatively, as it turned out, but with a round figure that seized the imagination and was widely repeated: a ton of gold!

"GOLD! GOLD! GOLD! GOLD!" screamed an extra edition of the *P-I* that hit the streets as the *Portland*

John McGraw, former governor of Washington state who left office in 1896, was among the first wave of gold-seekers headed north when word of the Klondike strike reached Seattle. McGraw retained his interest in Alaska and several years later was involved in construction of the Alaska Central Railway out of Seward. (Photo 121, Museum of History and Industry)

was tying up: "68 rich men on the Steamer *Portland;* STACKS OF YELLOW METAL!"

Five thousand people crowded Schwabacher's wharf when the *Portland* steamed in to Seattle, about 6 a.m. on July 17. Onlookers were electrified to see men staggering down the gangway with bags they could barely heft. As the indecorous sourdoughs reached the dock, one miner recalled, they were mobbed by reporters "who clung to us like limpets."

All morning, the people of Seattle poured onto the streets to discuss the fabulous news. By 9:30 a.m., downtown streets were so packed that some streetcars had to stop running. Half the men of Seattle drew up

schemes for rushing north. The other half schemed to outfit them.

Well before it docked, the *Portland's* return passage north was fully booked. Among the 148 ticketed passengers was former Gov. John McGraw, unseated in an election the year before. Doctors and lawyers, salesmen, clerks and clergymen quit their jobs and lit out for the Klondike. More than half the city's police officers and firemen left within a fortnight of the *Portland's* arrival. Seattle's mayor, Col. W.D. Wood, in San Francisco for a convention when the treasure ships came in, wired the city council to request a leave of absence. He soon raised $150,000, bought a steamship and formed the Seattle and Yukon Trading Co. In the first flush of gold fever, it seemed like a scheme that couldn't miss, although it was a move Wood lived to regret.

"Ho! For the Klondike!" was the slogan that beckoned in steamship and railway ads. Up and down the West Coast, across the continent and around the globe, a new and virulent strain of gold fever raged: Klondicitis, the newspapers called it, or simply Klondike fever.

Having hosted the first gold-ship from the Klondike, San Francisco was one center of the infection. "INEXHAUSTIBLE RICHES OF THE NORTHERN EL DORADO," trumpeted the *San Francisco Call* of July 20. "Official Verification of the Wonderful Gold Discoveries in the Klondyke District."

San Francisco was built on the California gold rush of nearly 50 years earlier, and it fully expected to cash in on the Klondike, too. It was home port of the Alaska Commercial Co., which still enjoyed a near monopoly on commerce up and down the Yukon River. It also boasted the only government assay office on the West Coast, where miners could be assured of receiving full and fair value for their mineral wealth.

Portland, Oregon, and Tacoma, Washington, hoped to capitalize, too, based on their ports and their railroad links to the east. Vancouver, British Columbia, tried to trade on its railroad connections and port — and the fact that it was in Canada, as was the gold. In Alaska, Juneau promoted its mining experience and its proximity to the gold fields. Even landlocked Edmonton, in Alberta, promoted the illusory advantages of its "all-Canadian overland backdoor route" to the riches. But it fell to Seattle to attract the lion's share of commerce with the Klondike and later Alaska stampedes, to its everlasting gain.

Competition was fierce among the cities, at least initially. San Francisco proclaimed its long history of outfitting miners and staged an exposition to show how to

After U.S. purchase of Alaska, the assets of the Russian American Co. were eventually absorbed by the Alaska Commercial Co., which for several years dominated commerce in the American Far North. The ACC had its headquarters on Sansome Street in San Francisco, where in a room on an upper floor the company stored furs collected by agents at its many trading posts in Alaska. The building was filled with the documents of Alaska's first half-century under U.S. control, and when the great earthquake and fire struck San Francisco in 1906, most of that history went up in smoke. (Photo FN-02584, California Historical Society, San Francisco)

mine. It promoted its fine hotels and restaurants and, for good measure, suggested that argonauts would be cheated in frontier Seattle.

Portland merchants claimed that they could outfit a miner for 10 percent less than it would cost in Seattle, a savings of at least $50. Some asserted, in a rather bold lie, that steamers for Alaska all left from Portland, according to William Spiedel, the Seattle author of *Sons of the Profits* (1967). Since Seattle was merely a stopover on the voyage north, they warned, the only way to be assured of a berth was to board at the start, in Portland.

Tacoma merchants made similar false claims that all ships originated in their port. They too fostered doubts about the honesty of their Puget Sound neighbors. "Tacoma sent phony stories out under the guise of news," Spiedel writes, "about prominent barons and dukes from Europe who said they planned to go to Tacoma to outfit rather than Seattle because they would get cheated in Seattle."

In British Columbia, promoters dispatched agents to Seattle to offer argonauts free transportation to Victoria and Vancouver. The Canadian Pacific Railroad slashed fares so that a transcontinental ticket cost $25, about a quarter of the United States rate. Since the Klondike was in Canada, Canadian boosters argued, gold-seekers who outfitted with them wouldn't pay a duty. Seattle merchants retaliated, Spiedel writes, by spreading their own mis-information "that Canadian bacon was wheat-fed and would not stand up under the moisture in the gold fields."

In Alaska, Juneau merchants made a mostly vain bid for a piece of the Klondike trade. "I liked Juneau's propaganda line best," Spiedel reveals. "Juneau pointed out that outfits in Seattle were stowed at the bottom of the ships' holds, while horses and mules were stowed just above them — and pee'd all over them for the three weeks' trip to Alaska."

Although Juneau didn't enjoy the boom that Seattle did from outfitting the Klondike stampeders, the town did experience modest commercial growth. Decker Bro's. promoted their services with the motto: "A Square Deal." (Photo PCA 87-1048 by Winter & Pond, Alaska State Library)

In the end, there was no contest. Seattle grabbed the bulk of the Klondike trade. As the U.S.' northernmost rail-port, it had good rail connections and an excellent harbor. It was closer to the Klondike than Tacoma or Portland, and was more than 600 miles closer than San Francisco. Finally, Seattle enjoyed one other decisive advantage: Seattle had Erastus Brainerd.

Brainerd was a handsome Connecticut Yankee, a Harvard-educated newspaperman and lover of the arts. He began in the news business as an editorial writer on the *New York World* then moved to the *Atlanta Constitution.* In 1890, Brainerd was with the *Philadelphia Press* when one of his friends bought the *Seattle Press* and persuaded the energetic Brainerd to go west to run it. A year later, Brainerd's friend bought the troubled Seattle *Times* and combined his two newspapers under Brainerd's editorship.

The U.S. economy, which had been sluggish since the mid-1880s, slumped into depression with the Panic of 1893. Part of the problem was the scarcity of gold. European countries had adopted a gold standard and demanded payments in gold, causing U.S. reserves of the precious metal to dwindle alarmingly. In the Pacific Northwest, logging mills closed, railroads and banks collapsed. The maritime industry suffered and unemployment soared.

The newly merged *Press-Times* lost money from the start. Given the grim economic climate, both advertising and readers were hard to come by. Nor did Brainerd's somewhat rarefied coverage of literature and the arts help. Brainerd finally resigned his editorship and took a job as state land commissioner, under Gov. John McGraw. When McGraw was turned out of office in 1896, Brainerd was turned out too.

Brainerd had difficulty finding work that suited him. He served as Paraguayan consul for a region covering Alaska, Washington, Oregon and Idaho, but that was not a full-time occupation. He was still in the job market when his ship, and Seattle's — the *Portland* — came in.

By the time of the Klondike strike, Seattle businesses had been trading with Alaska and outfitting prospectors for two decades. Some businesses, especially the steamship companies and outfitters, responded quickly to the outbreak of Klondike fever. But weeks passed before Seattle's business community pulled together an organized response.

Toward the end of August, the Chamber of Commerce met to discuss ways to ensure that Seattle reaped its share of the coming gold rush trade. In September, a subscription system was formalized to fund advertising and a public relations campaign. Businesses initially pledged a total of $990 a month for five months. Schwabacher Bros., a diverse mercantile concern, topped the list with a commitment of $75 a month. Five companies pledged $50 a month: Moran Bros. shipyard plus four outfitters, Cooper & Levy, Seattle Hardware, Fischer Bros. and MacDougall and Southwick. The kitty of just under $5,000 was later doubled.

Erastus Brainerd was put in charge of the campaign. At age 42, the failed frontier editor had found his calling. Brainerd knew most of the important magazine editors and newspapermen in the east. He understood advertising — and he appreciated what it could do. His plan was simple, to link two words in the minds of the American public: Seattle and Alaska. Overnight, Alaska meant gold. Soon, Seattle would mean Alaska.

Brainerd launched his campaign with a broadside. He advertised and wrote articles, passed information to newspapers and magazines. He directed letter-writing campaigns to public officials and newspapers. He put together guides to mining and Alaska and assembled photographic brochures. He was little encumbered by journalistic ethics, at least by modern standards. And he was tireless.

Seattle spent five times more on advertising than any competing city, indeed, easily more than all its competitors combined. It advertised in *McClure's, Cosmopolitan* and *Scribner's* magazines. It advertised in rural papers with a total readership of 10 million and in

Erastus Brainerd, a New Englander who had had an up-and-down career in journalism, found Seattle during the Klondike rush ready to embrace his promotional skills. The Seattle Chamber of Commerce hired Brainerd to put Seattle's name in front of gold-seekers and to launch a campaign to get the government to open an assay office in the city. Employing all manner of schemes, Brainerd did more than most to ensure that Seattle profited from the gold rush. (Photo 2699, Special Collections, University of Washington Libraries)

the largest national newspapers. Brainerd wrote articles for eastern newspapers and magazines, including *Harper's Weekly*, and then cited the articles and quoted himself (unattributed) in new articles.

Brainerd drafted a series of form letters about Seattle and the Klondike and supplied them to businessmen whose newly arrived employees signed them and mailed them to their hometown newspapers. He employed stenographers to write personal letters to the governor of every state and to the mayor of every city in America of 5,000 population or more. The letters described what gold-seekers would require in Alaska and urged people to write to Seattle for more information. They earnestly requested estimates of the number of people from their towns or states who would go to Alaska, so that Seattle could prepare to properly outfit them.

Every library in the country was sent brochures with photos of the Klondike, Alaska and Seattle. For Christmas in 1897, special photographs were sent as gifts to heads of South American republics and to every monarch in Europe. Whenever a response came in, Brainerd cranked out another press release. The best response of all came when the German Kaiser's staff destroyed a photo packet, fearing it was a bomb. Newspapers the world over ran the story and once more, the connection was reinforced: Alaska and Seattle.

Perhaps Brainerd's boldest scheme involved William D. Jenkins, Washington state's secretary of state. He convinced Jenkins to sign a letter on official letterhead to accompany a document sent to governors and mayors with the sober title, "Distance, Dangers and Probable Expense." The document discussed the difficulties and logistics of traveling to the gold fields and inquired where prospective argonauts planned to outfit and how they could "be contacted with proper information before they leave." It urged officials to convene press conferences to share this vital information from Washington State — and some of them did. To cap things off, the U.S. Department of State helpfully forwarded copies of Brainerd's — er, Jenkins' — document to 15 foreign governments.

Seattle: Gateway to Gold

There was gold to be made in supplying gold-seekers, as businessmen from Dawson's Joe Ladue on south clearly saw. Claiming one's fortune in the Klondike required cash up front.

Arthur Dietz, an argonaut from New York, wrote that "no one could start unless he had at least $500 and many had more than $5000."

Dietz was physical director of the Young Men's Christian Association in New York City when he contracted gold fever, according to his memoir, *Mad Rush for Gold in Frozen North* (1914). He advertised in the *New York Herald* for a few partners to form a Klondike mining company, according to his memoir. "The next morning the postman brought me no fewer than forty letters, and more during the day. They came from men in every station of life — clerks, policemen, firemen, and in three instances women wanted to join our party and claimed to have sufficient funds."

Dietz organized a party of 18 men, including his brother-in-law, who abandoned a medical practice in Brooklyn. The group also included a mineralogist, two civil engineers, two policemen and a factory superintendent. The men met every Sunday for four months to prepare, reading books on the Arctic. They trained four large dogs to haul sleds and attracted much publicity in local newspapers before they finally boarded a train for Seattle.

It took Dietz' party nine days to cross the continent. "At that time the city of Seattle was a maelstrom of raving humanity driven half insane by the desire for gold," Dietz wrote. "Between 1800 and 2000 people from all over the world were there clamoring for transportation to Alaska when there was none. Money was plentiful and fabulous prices were asked for everything. Every scheme, legal and illegal, mostly illegal, ever devised by mortals to separate a man from his money was run 'wide open.'"

Dietz himself was fooled into buying 100 pounds of "evaporated eggs." "The agent poured some of the yellow

The Australia *leaves Seattle, headed north. Of the thousands of gold-seekers who sailed from West Coast ports, only about 40,000 made it to Dawson during the boom years of the late 1890s, and many of those arrived too late to find any gold. (Photo 531 by A.H. Wilse, Special Collections, University of Washington Libraries)*

powder out and cooked it," he recalled. "It tasted like scrambled eggs which indeed it was, but it was all a sleight-of-hand trick for the stuff we paid for was yellow corn meal. Although we were very careful, many of the supplies we bought were worthless."

At least 10 routes to the Klondike were attempted, but three were predominant. One was an all-water route, by ship across the Gulf of Alaska and through the Bering Sea to St. Michael, then by riverboat up the Yukon River to Dawson. The Yukon began to freeze in late September, and only a handful of stampeders attempting the all-water route reached Dawson in 1897.

The other two major routes were by ship up the Inside Passage of the Alaska Panhandle to either Skagway or Dyea. From Skagway, a trail led inland through White Pass. From Dyea, three miles northwest of Skagway, another trail crossed Chilkoot Pass. Both mountain trails descended to the headwaters of the Yukon River, at lakes Lindeman and Bennett. Gold-seekers built boats on the lakes and negotiated some 550 river-miles to Dawson.

More than 90 percent of the stampeders the first year passed through Skagway or Dyea. Some 5,000 lit out across White Pass, but a remarkable 22,000 stampeders tackeled Chilkoot Pass during the winter of 1897-98. Few made it to Dawson before winter closed in. Thousands camped on the frozen shores of lakes Lindeman and Bennett until spring, when they built rough-hewn boats and dashed to Dawson.

Images of the human chain inching up the last steep pitch to the summit of Chilkoot Pass remain the predominant icon of the Klondike gold rush. What the photographs cannot show is the fact that gold-seekers had to conquer the mountain passes repeatedly. North West Mounted Police at the top refused access to Canada to any stampeder who was not outfitted with food and supplies for a year. Adequate food alone weighed more

than 1,000 pounds. The final ascent up the Chilkoot, an icy 35-degree slope to the 3,500-foot pass, was too steep for horses. To shuttle a prospector's supplies over the mountains meant dozens of trips on foot. The Mounties may have been cursed by some gold-seekers, but in their implacable insistence on the rules, the Mounties surely prevented mass tragedy along the trail to Dawson.

A Klondike outfit complete enough to satisfy the Mounties cost between $500 and $1,000 and weighed between 1,500 and 2,000 pounds. Recommended staples included 350 pounds of flour, 150 pounds of bacon, 100 pounds of beans and 100 pounds of sugar. There were rice, rolled oats, coffee and tea, plus dried foods such as egg yolks, fruits and vegetables. There were blankets and heavy woolen clothing, and perhaps a new-fangled, specially designed sleeping bag. There was a tent, utensils, tools and mining equipment such as axes, saws and picks, perhaps a sheet-iron stove and a sled. There may have been a wheelbarrow. A medicine kit included a source of vitamin C, typically lime juice capsules or citric acid powder, plus plasters and bandages and some sort of antiseptic.

Some stampeders brought unorthodox items. A hundred turkeys were herded through White Pass by a pair of entrepreneurs who intended to sell them in Dawson. One couple hauled a small portable piano over the Chilkoot trail. They protected the sounding board by wrapping it in yarn, which the woman knit into sweaters and then sold. Less amusing were the useless, often ungainly and sometimes dangerous items sold to gullible gold-seekers: foldable boats that leaked or stoves said to burn any fuel but that tended to incinerate tents as well.

Advice on the proper Klondike outfit was bewilderingly abundant. Booklets and pamphlets offering the recommendations of "experienced Alaskan miners" were snapped up by anxious argonauts. Tips were freely offered in magazine and newspaper articles about life in the mining camps, and in the advertisements of outfitters, with which West Coast papers were filled.

Even advice on just where to find gold in the Klondike could be had in Seattle. An ad in the *Seattle Daily Times* on Feb. 17, 1898, promoted the services of "Mrs. Lenont, reliable spiritual and business medium; information of gold localities by 'White Bear,' her Alaskan guide. Public circles under spirit control Monday, Thursday, Friday, 8 p.m."

Another ad in the same paper, the same day, urged gold-seekers to "Consult Raymond, Boy Medium, about Klondike. Truthful predictions, independent slate writings; circles Wednesday, Friday and Sunday evenings."

If mediums were not your medium, perhaps something in a rodent would be of interest. The Trans-Alaska Gopher Co. offered gophers trained to tunnel for the precious metal.

Of course, there was plenty of legitimate commerce with gold-seekers in Seattle and other gateway cities. During the first month after the *Portland's* fateful landfall, merchants in Seattle outfitted prospectors with supplies worth $325,000. By fall, about 1,000 locals had left for the North, and thousands of others stricken with Klondike fever were flocking to Seattle on the Great Northern and Northern Pacific railroads.

A good share of the outfitting was done by Cooper & Levy, Pioneer Outfitters. Photographs of the period show men sitting on wooden crates and sleds and leaning against canvas sacks stacked 6 feet high in front of the outfitters' store on First Avenue, next to the Northern Pacific ticket office.

Cooper & Levy had been feeding, supplying and outfitting lumber camps and rural retailers since 1891. Increasingly, the partners' customers had included gold-seekers bound for the North. In the July 17 morning

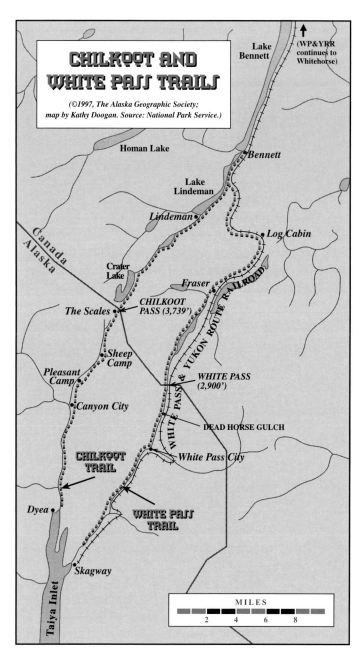

CHILKOOT AND WHITE PASS TRAILS

(©1997, The Alaska Geographic Society; map by Kathy Doogan. Source: National Park Service.)

newspaper, the very edition which heralded the arrival of the *Portland*, an astute Cooper & Levy ad cautioned, "Don't get excited and rush away half-prepared. You're going to a country where grub can be more valuable than gold, and frequently can't be had at any price. We can fit you out quicker and better than any firm in town. We have had lots of experience and know how to pack and what to furnish."

The $325,000 in goods sold by Seattle outfitters during the first month of the stampede was about equal to their annual trade before the rush. Their sales in 1899 jumped to about $10 million. Businesses that supplied the outfitters prospered as well. A Seattle inventor designed and patented a sleeping bag, which sold well to argonauts. Companies sprang up to produce dried staples and other foods: dried peaches, apples and currants,

potatoes, onions and soups. A factory in Kent produced 3,000 cans of evaporated milk per day. The business's founder, E.A. Stuart, made a fortune from his Carnation Milk Products Co.

Still other businesses cashed in on the gold-rush trade. Shipyards and steamship lines, banks and even railroads were rescued from the hard times that followed the Panic of '93.

At the start of the stampede, Seattle was served by four steamship lines with Alaska connections. Each scrambled to put additional vessels into operation on Alaska routes. New steamship lines sprang up and the price of passage to Skagway or Dyea jumped. Even so, the ships were full. Hauling freight, plus the ton or so of each stampeder's outfit, ships were often dangerously overloaded.

Anything that could float, and much that could not, was pressed into service in the North. Shipyards struggled to refit and repair old vessels. The task was made more difficult by the loss of labor to the gold fields. Somehow, the marine labor force was doubled, according to historian Scott Eckberg. Then it was tripled.

Orders flowed in to build steamboats for Yukon River trade. The Moran Bros. shipyard alone employed 375

When word of the Klondike strike reached Seattle, the local chamber of commerce rallied its members to subscribe to an advertising campaign aimed at convincing gold-seekers that they should purchase their outfits in Seattle. Cooper & Levy pledged $50 a month toward the effort. The Northern Pacific and Great Northern railroads sought to profit also by carrying would-be gold kings from the East Coast and Midwest to jumping off points in the Pacific Northwest. (Photo 401, Museum of History and Industry)

men in constructing a dozen riverboats. By mid-January, 1898, Puget Sound shipyards had orders for more than 60 craft for Yukon service, half of them barges for freight. "This represented a tonnage of 22,000," Eckberg reports, "and a passenger capacity of 10,500."

A dozen Yukon River steamers await finishing touches at the Moran Bros. Co. in Seattle in 1898. The vessels were 175 feet long, 35 feet wide but only 6 1/2 feet deep to accommodate the sometimes-shallow channels of the river. (Photo 1091, Museum of History and Industry)

Ebb Tide of the Klondike

Anticipating an influx of gold from Yukon Territory and Alaska, Seattle interests renewed their bid for a federal government assay office in their city. Ever since the Juneau strike of 1880, gold had been trickling, then flowing, south from Alaska. In 1894, $2 million in Alaska gold had been brought out through Seattle. A year later, the figure was $3 million, then $4 million in 1896. It was in response to this that Tom and Salome Lippy had gone north in March 1896. Thousands of gold-seekers had by

then passed through Seattle and many were awaiting passage to Alaska.

Gold in nuggets or dust is typically between 50 percent and 80 percent pure. A miner, consequently, never knows just how much gold he has until it is assayed or analyzed. Banks were perfectly willing to perform such tests, but miners were never quite sure they were getting all that was due them. The safest way, many felt, was to have their raw gold tested by a government assay office.

Klondikers in a variety of dress pose outside the Alaska Commercial Co. store at Dawson. (Photo PCA 277-1-207, Alaska State Library)

And the one nearest Alaska was in San Francisco.

In April 1897, while George Carmack and his newly wealthy neighbors were cooling their heels in Dawson awaiting the thaw, the Trustees of the Seattle Chamber of Commerce sent an appeal to Congress asking that a government assay office be established in Seattle. Four days after the *Portland* off-loaded nearly 2 tons of gold, the Chamber renewed its effort, citing the "startling events of the last few days." The Chamber pointed out that West Coast gold production far outpaced that in the east, yet there were three U.S. Assay Offices on the Atlantic seaboard and only one on the Pacific coast. Furthermore, the Chamber said, Klondike miners had brought their gold 6,000 miles to Seattle and it was wrong to force them to haul it another 800 miles to "get upon it the only satisfactory statement of value — the certificate of the United States assayer."

The extra travel may have been inconvenient for miners, but for Seattle, it was downright bad business. It was as if the miners had paychecks that could only be cashed in California. Local businessmen wanted the miners to sell their gold in Seattle, figuring they might stick around and spend or invest their wealth locally.

Congress ignored the Chamber's plea. When Washington's Sen. John Wilson took it up with the director of the U.S. Mint, he was told that there was no need for an assay office in Seattle.

In the spring of 1898, the Chamber's patience ran out. They pooled some money, put Erastus Brainerd in charge and instructed him to work their will.

Brainerd soon discovered that Congress had appropriated money for an assay office in South Dakota, but that the office had never been opened and the money had never been spent. He knew that Congressmen would ask how he proposed to fund Seattle's assay office, and *voila!* He had found an answer!

The next problem was how to keep the bill from getting lost in the crush of legislative affairs. Thanks to the gold rush, Alaska had been rediscovered and Congress faced some 600 bills related to the District. Brainerd latched onto a sympathetic Congressman in Charles Stone, of Pennsylvania. Stone was a member of the House Committee overseeing the U.S. Mint. He also happened to have a brother in business in Seattle.

The campaign masterminded by Brainerd and Stone heated up a bit when Juneau and Portland launched bids for assay offices of their own. But the interlopers' efforts were deflected and on May 16, 1898, Stone's bill prevailed by a vote of 128 to 17. The Senate had already approved the bill without debate and the U.S. Assay Office in Seattle was soon in business.

The rush to the Klondike was furious but relatively short-lived. It peaked in 1898, the year after the *Excelsior* and the *Portland* brought out the first gold. In July of 1899, the White Pass and Yukon Railway was completed to Lake Bennett. A year later, the railroad linked coastal Skagway with Whitehorse on the Yukon River, ameliorating the upper Yukon's dreadful isolation.

But the ebb tide of the Klondike was far from the end of the story. Indeed, for Alaska, it was more nearly the beginning. As prospectors by the thousands swarmed westward in search of new gold fields, the finds came in quick succession. In September 1898, gold was found near Nome, on Anvil Creek. The following July, the sand on the beach in Nome was discovered to contain the sought-after yellow metal.

It was the Klondike all over again as gold-seekers flung up a tent community in Nome. In a single week

Buck Choquette found gold on some of the Stikine River's bars in 1861. In 1873-74 the area experienced a mini-stampede when gold was found in the Cassiar district of British Columbia. Glenora, never more than a string of tents and modest log buildings along the Stikine River, peaked during the Klondike rush. With virtual abandonment of the Teslin Lake trail to the Klondike in favor of the Chilkoot Pass route, and with establishment of Telegraph Creek as the primary head of navigation on the Stikine River, Glenora quickly died. (B.C. Provincial Archives)

during August 1899, 8,000 prospectors fled Dawson and stampeded down the Yukon, according to Klondike expert Pierre Berton. Ironically, the same week a handful of men staggered into Dawson. They were the last of the argonauts who had set out from Edmonton two years before via the "all-Canadian overland" route. Theirs was truly the "back door route" to the Klondike.

When word of the Nome phenomenon reached Seattle and San Francisco, another feverish rush ensued. This time, ocean steamships obligingly carried argonauts all the way to the gold field. Thirteen miles of beach was staked as rockers and sluice boxes reclaimed riches from the ocean's golden shore. Other finds were made on creeks outside Nome. The district produced $4 million in gold annually for several years.

In 1902, gold was found in the Tanana Valley, in Alaska's interior. Fairbanks grew to serve the region. It was the first major town in Alaska not on the coast. By 1908, 3,500 people lived in Fairbanks and as many as

15,000 were scattered in mining camps throughout the surrounding hills.

Gold was found in Innoko in 1906 and Iditarod in 1908. By one count, between a strike along the upper Koyukuk in 1893 and a 1914 find in Livengood, Alaska had 34 gold stampedes of various magnitudes.

Gold production peaked in 1906, when miners extracted more than 1 million troy ounces. The value of the metal was $22 million, or three times the price of Alaska's purchase from Russia 39 years earlier.

The assay office for which Brainerd and the Chamber of Commerce had lobbied so vigorously operated for 10 years. During that time, it bought most of the gold from the Klondike, Nome and other stampedes. Gold worth

roughly $175 million flowed south through Seattle. Close to $100 million of that may have been spent or invested in Seattle.

The Alaska gold rushes came at a crucial time. They ended the depression of the not-so-Gay Nineties and provided business and capital that helped fuel a spurt of growth from which Seattle emerged as Puget Sound's dominant city. In 1890, Seattle and Tacoma had been rivals of comparable size. But by 1900, Seattle was more than twice as large as its would-be rival and by 1910, Seattle was more than five times the size of Tacoma. It had also outgrown Portland to become the largest city in the Pacific Northwest. To find a larger city, one had to go 600 miles south to San Francisco or 1,500 miles east to metropolitan Minneapolis.

■ ■ ■

As important as the gold rush was, it would be easy to overestimate its impact on Seattle. The city responded to the influx of capital because it was primed for growth.

FACING PAGE: *Alaska Commercial Co. executive officers (left to right) Gustave Niebaum, Lewis Gerstle (Vice President) and Louis Sloss (President) meet in the bookkeeping room of the company's main office at 310 Sansome St., San Francisco. (Courtesy of Western Jewish History Center of the Judah L. Magnes Museum, Ernest Lilienthal Collection)*

RIGHT: *Like "peas and beans" is how Richard Harris, shown here, described the gold he and partner Joe Juneau found in a basin in the mountains behind Juneau in 1880. Their find, on Oct. 3, was the first major gold strike in Alaska. (Photo PCA 87-2372 by Winter & Pond, Alaska State Library)*

Blessed by geography, transcontinental rail links, steamship lines, healthy shipyards and a strong mercantile sector, Seattle had already outpaced Tacoma at the start of the stampede and had grown into a city of 65,000. After a catastrophic fire in 1889, the city's downtown had been rebuilt in brick and stone. There were banks

and municipal buildings, hotels, department stores and small factories, fish and meat markets, groceries, clothing stores and laundries. There were mansions and boarding houses, energetic working-class areas and immigrant neighborhoods teeming with Chinese, Japanese, Filipinos and Swedes. During the preceding decade or two, Seattle had forged economic ties with Alaska, handling millions of cases of canned salmon. Along with San Francisco, Seattle had supplied mining camps and merchants in the Juneau gold district and had even sent summer tourists to Wrangell, Sitka and other points along the Inside Passage.

Other West Coast cities benefited from the rush for Alaska gold, too. The San Francisco-based Alaska Commercial Co. expanded operations along the Yukon River and across Alaska. Portland and Tacoma captured shares of the outfitting and transportation trade, and their shipyards bustled with work on vessels bound for the North. Vancouver, B.C., nearly doubled in population during the gold rush period.

In 1909, Seattle paid tribute to her links with the North by hosting the Alaska-Yukon-Pacific Exposition. The impetus for the exposition had come in 1905 when a Seattle businessman put together an exhibit of Alaska products and artifacts for the Lewis and Clark Exposition in Portland. Not to be outdone, Seattle's version of a trade exposition grew into a full-blown World's Fair, with exhibitions from countries around the Pacific Rim.

The site of the fair was the still-rural University of Washington campus, part of which was logged to make room for the Arctic Circle, a group of seven, white, neo-classical buildings surrounding a basin and fountain. Most of the structures were temporary, although the University did inherit at least one large building. The fair's other attraction was the Pay Streak, a gaudy amusement park complete with exotic sideshows. One of these was a group of Igorots, from a tribe in the Philippine jungle,

whose loinclothes stirred a protest among the more staid of the city's Edwardian moralists.

The grounds of the AYP were laid out by the Olmsted brothers, sons of Frederick Law Olmsted, the designer of New York's Central Park. The Olmsteds had previously designed a system of boulevards and winding parkways for Seattle, substantial portions of which came into being and which help to define the city's green character today.

During its 108-day run, nearly 4 million people attended the AYP, including President William Howard Taft. Seattle presented itself to the world through the fair, and the young city cleaned itself up for the occasion. Much of what remained from the wild and roaring days of the early stampede was erased as Seattle declared its dream of becoming a world-class city, embracing the varied cultures of the Pacific Rim.

Unlike Seattle, Erastus Brainerd did not cash in on the rush for Alaska gold. But it was not for want of trying. One of his few failed campaigns was an effort to get himself appointed U.S. Consul in Dawson City. A dozen U.S. Senators, nine governors and scores of influential citizens urged the State Department to open a consulate in Dawson and to send Brainerd, alas, to no avail.

Brainerd eventually went to Alaska where he worked rather unsuccessfully as a "mining consultant." He returned to Seattle and, in 1904, became editor of the *Post-Intelligencer*. He died in Tacoma, at age 67, on Christmas Day, 1922.

Neither of the newspapers he had edited carried news of Erastus Brainerd's death on the front page. His obituaries were silent on his role in making Seattle the gateway to Alaska gold. When Murray Morgan wrote *Skid Road*, his classic portrait of Seattle, in 1951, he asked the *Post-Intelligencer* librarian for the newspaper's clippings on Erastus Brainerd. "Brainerd? Brainerd?" the librarian asked. "Is he a communist or something?"

Thanks to Morgan's book and others since, Erastus Brainerd's name is better known today. "This author and editor," Morgan writes of Brainerd, "whose friends considered him to be touched with genius, probably did more than any other individual to annex the Territory of Alaska to the City of Seattle." ■

This view of the grounds of the 1909 Alaska-Yukon-Pacific Exposition on the University of Washington campus in Seattle was taken from a balloon one-quarter mile above the earth. The exposition celebrated Seattle's connection with the North and its ties to the gold rush. (Photo 14138, Museum of History and Industry)

FEVER IN THE NORTH

Traders on the Yukon

The first problem faced by argonauts in 1897 was the first objective of any gold rush: rushing to the gold. Transportation in Alaska and the Yukon was woefully lacking. Travel to and within the district was usually arduous and invariably time-consuming.

To begin with, the expanse of the sparsely settled and largely undeveloped territory was daunting. Alaska comprises 586,400 square miles, more than the combined areas of Idaho, Washington, Oregon, California, Nevada and Utah. There are imposing mountain ranges with 19 peaks higher than 14,000 feet, including Mount McKinley, North America's tallest mountain. Alaska has more than 30,000 miles of shoreline, more than the entire eastern seaboard of the U.S.

It is not only Alaska's breadth and topography that impede travel. Huge glaciers and ice fields guard much of its southern coast, while its northern realm is a vast tundra plain dotted with wetlands and lakes. Alaska's climate can intimidate, too, from the rain forest of the Panhandle to the foggy, wind-swept Aleutians to the frigid arctic coast. And there are countless swift rivers to cross or negotiate, including the mighty Yukon, one of the world's longest waterways.

The Yukon River is the primordial artery that flows through the heart of Alaska. It drains more than half of the state. It arises just 15 miles from the sea, in rainfall and snow melt that drains into interconnected alpine lakes on the northeastern side of British Columbia's coastal mountains. The river flows to the northwest past Whitehorse, past Dawson and into Alaska until it touches the Arctic Circle. There, at Fort Yukon, the river picks up its longest tributary, the Porcupine River. It turns and flows southwestward, collecting other tributaries including the Tanana and the Koyukuk as it wends its way to Norton Sound. Toward the end of its journey, as

FACING PAGE: *North West Mounted Police gather at the first Customs House built at the summit of Chilkoot Pass in February 1898. (Pringle Collection, courtesy of Pat Roppel)*

A decade before George Carmack made his discovery in the Klondike, the Treadwell Mine, on the slopes of Douglas Island across Gastineau Channel from Juneau, was showing signs of the bonanza it was to become. Carpenter John Treadwell and partners from San Francisco had consolidated several claims on the island and formed Alaska Mining and Milling Co. Treadwell eventually sold out to other developers, but the complex continued to produce phenomenal wealth. By one account, the Treadwell claims yielded $67 million worth of pure gold. (Courtesy of Pat Roppel)

it nears the sea again after some 2,000 miles of rambling, the Yukon spreads wide the fingers of a great delta, more than 60 miles across.

Concomitant with the peaceful transfer of Alaska to the United States in 1867, the Russian American Co. sold all of its holdings to an American firm. The Alaska Commercial Co. took control of all of the trading posts, warehouses, ships and inventories of its Russian predecessor in Alaska trade.

The ACC wasted little time in bringing change to trade on the Yukon River. In June 1869, the ACC ship *Commodore* arrived at St. Michael with a small stern-wheeler lashed to her deck. The 50-foot *Yukon* was the first steamboat on the river.

Flying the American flag and firing a volley of guns in salute, the *Yukon* steamed from St. Michael on July 4, 1869, according to Barry C. Anderson. "Picking her way through channels that had never before been navigated by anything larger than a canoe, she reached Nulato 16 days later and Fort Yukon on July 31," Anderson reported in *Lifeline to the Yukon: A History of Yukon River Navigation* (1983).

The U.S. Army had sent Capt. Charles P. Raymond aboard the *Yukon* to ascertain the location of Fort Yukon with regard to the Alaska-Canada boundary. Raymond found that the Hudson's Bay post was some 80 miles inside U.S. territory. He took possession of the fort for the United States. A new day had dawned on the Yukon.

For 10 years, the *Yukon* was the sole steamboat on its namesake river. Each summer, after the ice went out, it would deliver supplies to trading posts, trappers and miners along the river well into Yukon Territory. The *Yukon* returned bearing bundles of fur, ore samples and the odd passenger. The short navigation season usually permitted a single round-trip, as the Yukon is freely navigable only about four months a year.

Important figures in the development of mining and commerce along the river now began to enter the country. In 1873, three of these reached Fort Yukon, all by descending the Porcupine. Arthur Harper was a restless Irish prospector and trapper. Leroy Napoleon McQuesten, known as Jack, and Al Mayo, a former circus acrobat, had been prospecting in British Columbia when they learned that the U.S. had bought Russian America. They determined to have a look and spent several years making their way there across Canada by hand-made canoe, raft and boat.

Of the three off-and-on partners, Harper was the most devoted prospector. He sought gold wherever he went and found some on the Fortymile, Sixtymile, Tanana and Klondike rivers, but never enough to make him settle down and mine.

McQuesten and Mayo took work from the ACC in 1874, and established their first trading post on the Yukon that year, six miles below the Klondike River. Fort Reliance became the reference point for later development along the upper Yukon: the Twelvemile, Fortymile and Sixtymile rivers were named because of their distance from Fort Reliance.

In 1875, Harper, McQuesten and Mayo all became independent traders working on commission for the ACC. They managed trading posts and also operated the *Yukon*. Often, one of them would captain the steamer

Even prior to the Klondike discoveries prospectors had poked among the gravels of streambeds throughout the middle and upper Yukon. Several tributaries near Eagle caught the attention of prospectors and small-scale mining operators. This miner checks his sluice to see if any color has been trapped among the riffles. (Photo 55, Stout Neg., BLM, Anchorage Museum)

and act as his own fireman, pilot, engineer and deckhand.

In 1879, a second sternwheeler began to ply the Yukon. The tiny *St. Michael* was put into service by the Western Fur and Trading Co., in competition with the ACC. Three years later, a wealthy prospector named Ed Schieffelin assembled a third steamer at St. Michael, to facilitate his search for gold.

After the discovery of gold near Juneau in 1880, the attention of Schieffelin and other argonauts had turned increasingly toward Alaska. Whispers of gold were seeping through the mountains from the interior. In 1878, a mysterious prospector named George Holt had appeared

Children from Miss Padock's classes perform for the townsfolk at Ruby in 1916. No doubt some of the youngsters are offspring of the golden gamblers who rushed up and down Alaska's interior rivers in response to word of the latest strike. Gold was discovered in the Ruby area on the Yukon River in 1907. Initial response to the strike on Ruby Creek was lackluster, but four years later a second strike on nearby Long Creek aroused enough interest that miners were drawn to the area and the town of Ruby was founded. (Photo PCA 277-4-118, Alaska State Library)

in Sitka bearing two gold nuggets he said were given to him by a Native in the upper Yukon.

At the time, the mountain passes that were to become the gateway to the Klondike were jealously guarded by Chilkoot sentinels. The Chilkoots were protecting their trade with the Natives of the interior, over whom they exerted considerable control. They were Tlingits, short, powerfully built men with thin black mustaches and beards, able to pack 150 pounds or more across the mountain passes. In 1852, the Chilkoots had attacked and burned Fort Selkirk, driving the Hudson's Bay Co. to abandon their outpost for nearly 30 years. Yet somehow, despite the Chilkoot sentries, George Holt had become the first white man to enter the upper Yukon valley through the icy coastal mountains.

Holt's report stirred Sitka, especially the prospectors who had drifted to Alaska's capital from British Columbia's gold fields. Three prospectors who tried to follow Holt's route in 1879 were turned back. In 1880, Capt. L.A. Beardslee of the U.S. Navy convinced the Chilkoots to let 19 prospectors through the coastal mountains. They were brought up Taiya Inlet aboard a gunboat and deposited near the foot of Chilkoot Pass. With a small military escort and a Coast and Geodetic Survey scientist, the miners hiked through the pass into the upper Yukon drainage.

This was the unlocking of the overland route to the Yukon. From a handful of prospectors, the Chilkoot Trail was traversed by increasing numbers of white men from 1880 onward. Nor were the Chilkoots altogether displeased: They charged a fee to pack outfits over the mountains, and when the Klondike stampede broke, their price soared as high as a dollar a pound. Like the merchants of Seattle and the magnates of the steamship lines, the Chilkoots mined the miners and made a fortune without panning an ounce of gold.

Quest for Gold:
From Fortymile to Circle City

Ed Schieffelin was intrigued by rumors of gold in Alaska, but it was not the Chilkoot Trail that beckoned to him. Schieffelin had discovered a mountain of silver and gold in Arizona and had founded the town of Tombstone. He was a millionaire, but his fortune never dampened his fever for gold. The lifelong prospector had pored over maps and evolved a theory he wanted to test. It seemed to him that a band of precious minerals must run from Cape Horn up the mountainous Andean spine of South America, through North America's Rocky Mountains and then in a great curving arc through Alaska and on into Asia. Somewhere, he reasoned, the golden belt must cross the mighty Yukon. A man in a steamboat could ascend the river until he found it.

In 1882, Schieffelin assembled a party to test his theory. At St. Michael, they pieced together a small but serviceable steamer, aptly named the *New Racket*. Author Barry Anderson describes her: "With her small hull occupied almost entirely by boiler and engine, she was reputed to be the ugliest vessel ever to ply the Yukon. Leaking steam from every joint and belching an exhaust that could be heard for miles, she lived up to her rather unusual name."

Schieffelin spent one season prospecting on the Yukon. He got as far as Rampart, nearly 800 miles upstream, where the river has cut an impressive gorge through surrounding hills. In the gravel of Rampart, Schieffelin found just enough "color" to convince him that he had discovered the gold belt he sought. But he had found the river bleak and forbidding, the country wild and remote. After wintering at Tanana Station, Schieffelin's party was discouraged and departed for St. Michael, never to return.

The *New Racket* did return. Schieffelin sold it to

McQuesten, Harper and Mayo and the trio used it for trade, passenger transport and various ventures of their own. The vessel survived on the river until the late 1880s but eventually wound up a victim of ice. A similar fate claimed the ACC's *Yukon*, the original steamboat on the river.

From the beginning, running steamboats in Alaska was a risky affair. There were rocks and rapids, shoals and sandbars and confusing, shifting, multiple braided channels. There were floods, logs and sweeps, fallen trees overhanging the banks that were apt to sweep unsuspecting boaters into the water. And there was ice.

The breakup of ice on the Yukon each spring is a spectacular event. Ice begins to move first in the upper river and in some tributaries, usually in mid-May. With a grating and crashing, slabs of ice the size of houses jostle and plow downstream with immense force. Because the ice downstream may still be intact, ice jams are common, damming the river and backing up floodwater to a depth of several feet. Dozens of villages along the Yukon have been flooded during spring breakup, some of them repeatedly. The ice on Norton Sound is the last to go, persisting as long as four weeks after the Yukon is clear.

In later years, steel-hulled riverboats could survive being frozen in during winter. For wooden-hulled boats, wintering over was always a peril. To avoid being crushed by great floes of ice during breakup, riverboat captains sometimes sought shallow, back-water sloughs to winter their boats. By stoking the boiler, a layer of water could be maintained around the hull. Ice beneath the boat was more difficult to affect, however, and sometimes a boat remained frozen fast to the bottom while rising flood waters overtopped the deck and sank the boat in place.

By 1886, McQuesten, Harper and Mayo were busy supplying and trading with some 200 prospectors who had entered Yukon Territory. Most had come over Chilkoot Pass and had worked their way down the Yukon to the mouth of the Stewart River, where they had struck gold. About $100,000 in gold was reclaimed from the sand bars of the Stewart in 1886.

One of many photographers who came north to document the various gold stampedes, Eric A. Hegg traveled along the Yukon in his boat. For 20 years Hegg explored Yukon Territory and Alaska, operating in Dyea, Dawson, Nome and Cordova. (Photo 338 by E.A. Hegg, Special Collections Division, University of Washington Libraries)

On July 24, 1914, Jay Livengood and N.E. "Teddy" Hudson discovered gold in an unnamed tributary of the Tolovana River, 50 miles northwest of Fairbanks. The creek was later named after Livengood, as was the settlement that grew there during the winter of 1914-15. By 1916 the Livengood camp had 250 residents, including 48 women. The population began declining in 1920. This photo, probably taken in the early 1930s, shows Teddy Hudson with a pan of gold, at the time worth $2,200. Hudson died in Fairbanks in 1952 at age 86. (R.L. Frost, U.S. Weather Bureau)

That winter, Harper urged two prospectors to try the Fortymile River, another 100 miles down the Yukon. They found coarse gold, rich enough to draw prospectors flocking. They came first from the Stewart River gold fields, then from the far side of Chilkoot Pass. The Fortymile stampede was underway.

By 1890, the camp at Fortymile was the largest settlement on the Yukon River. There were 200 log cabins, six saloons, two blacksmiths, stores and a self-styled opera house featuring dance-hall girls from San Francisco.

At first, it was impossible to supply all the Fortymile miners with enough food to last the winter. About two-thirds of the camp's population was forced to go down river to St. Michael or over Chilkoot Pass in the fall, only to make the demanding return trip in the spring.

To meet the increasing demand, the ACC built the *Arctic* at St. Michael in 1889. By far the largest steamer on the Yukon at the time, the *Arctic* was 135 feet long by 30 feet abeam. On her maiden voyage, the winds of Norton Sound drove her onto some rocks and the *Arctic* sank. She was refloated and repaired in time to operate the following year, but without her anticipated provisions that first season, Fortymile faced starvation.

The ACC sent Native messengers 1,600 miles upriver to warn the imperiled miners. The chill of October was in the air when dozens of Fortymilers crowded aboard the *New Racket* for a late run down river. The little steamer got caught in the ice 190 miles from St. Michael. The passengers disembarked and tramped to safety on foot.

With the need for additional riverboats on the Yukon came competition for the Alaska Commercial Co. The North American Trading and Transportation Co. formed in 1892, with backing from Chicago investors including meat-packing mogul Michael Cudahy. Mastermind of NAT&T was John Jerome Healy, a tough, formidable frontiersman. Healy had been a sheriff in Montana cattle country as well as a hunter, trapper, soldier, Indian scout, prospector, editor and whiskey-peddler.

When the Fortymile stampede began, Healy was running a trading post he had built on Taiya Inlet, at the foot of the Chilkoot Trail. He went to Chicago where he convinced an old friend, businessman Portus B. Weare, that the time was ripe to break the ACC's hold on Alaska. Weare approached other investors and Healy returned to build his new trading post, Fort Cudahy, across the river from Fortymile camp.

The NAT&T's first vessel, the *Portus B. Weare*, began operating in 1893. When Healy ran afoul of a miners' meeting ruling the same year, he wrote to another old frontier friend to call in the Mounties to tame the unruly boomtown.

Healy's old friend with the North West Mounted Police was Superintendent Samuel B. Steele. Steele agreed that the Canadian government needed a presence in the developing northern gold fields. In 1894, Inspector Charles Constantine opened an office in Fort Cudahy. The next year, a detachment of 20 Mounties joined him. It was

FACING PAGE: *At the height of the Klondike rush, pack animals were sometimes worth their weight in gold. But trails over the mountains to the upper Yukon drainage took their toll on the animals and made sections like Dead Horse Trail on the White Pass route an all-to-vivid reality. (Courtesy of Pat Roppel)*

these representatives of law and order with whom George Carmack was to file his momentous Klondike claims.

In 1895, the ACC added two new sternwheelers to their Yukon fleet, the *Alice* and the *Bella*, both built at St. Michael. The impetus for the fleet expansion came in part from NAT&T's challenge, but more important was the first rich strike in interior Alaska, on Birch Creek, in 1893.

Jack McQuesten had grubstaked the Creole prospectors who made the find, and the camp that sprang up was McQuesten's town. It was called Circle City, or just Circle, in the mistaken belief that it lay astride the Arctic Circle. In reality, Circle is some 50 miles south of the land of midnight sun.

In its brief heyday, just before the Klondike strike, Circle boasted an area population of around 1,200. In contrast to Fortymile, where Canadian law and order ruled, Circle was a roaring American Wild West town, with 28 saloons and eight dance halls. There were also two theaters, a music hall and a two-story Grand Opera House, where vaudeville shows alternated with Shakespearean plays. The *Chicago Daily Record* dispatched a correspondent to "the Paris of Alaska." John J. Healy's North American Trading opened a store in Circle in direct competition with McQuesten and the ACC.

McQuesten and the ACC had always operated on a basis of liberal credit. But by 1894, according to author Pierre Berton, the tab owed to McQuesten by miners in Circle City had reached $100,000.

An incident illustrating McQuesten's practices was observed by William Ogilvie, the Canadian surveyor who helped establish the Alaska-Canada boundary.

A miner who owed $700 came into McQuesten's store from the creeks. He had with him just $500.

"Oh, that's all right," McQuesten assured him. "Give us your five hundred and we'll credit you and let the rest stand till next clean-up."

"But, Jack, I want more stuff. How'm I going to get it?"

"We'll let you have it, same as we did before."

"But, damn it, Jack, I haven't had a spree yet."

McQuesten sent the man off to have his little spree. When he returned having spent everything, McQuesten calmly gave him $500 worth of supplies and sent him back to the creeks, carrying a $1,200 debt against him.

In August 1896, Fortymile had emptied after George Carmack's announcement of the Klondike strike. When the *Alice* called a fortnight later, those who hadn't left already piled aboard. They became the first stampeders to reach Dawson by steamer, on September 5.

In Circle, skepticism ran deeper. Rumors of the find floated slowly downriver before freeze-up, but they were frankly disbelieved. Shortly before Christmas, an ACC trader arrived from Dawson with a packet of mail and a quantity of gold. A saloon keeper read one letter aloud to a packed room. The writer reported having seen $150 in gold panned out in a single pan and opined that some miners were getting $1,000 a pan. The crowd roared. They had heard it all before. Two sourdoughs, however, received a separate letter from an old partner whom they were inclined to take seriously. They fitted up a dog-team and started upriver to check things out.

And the news kept coming. In January, more mail arrived. Saloon-keeper Harry Ash received a letter from a trusted friend. He tore it open, read it and announced to his patrons, according to Pierre Berton, "Boys, help yourself to the whole shooting match, I'm off to the Klondike!" Ash ripped off his apron and dashed out the door, leaving behind a room plunged into chaos.

The wider world still knew nothing of the Klondike strike, but within Yukon Territory and now in adjacent Alaska, the rush was on. Instantly the price of a sled dog in Circle jumped from around $50 to $250, then to $1,500. Circle citizens started across the ice, pulled by sled dogs or pulling their own sleds. On foot, it took about three weeks to cover the 200-plus river miles to Dawson. But when breakup arrived, the Paris of Alaska was a ghostly shell.

Berton writes of one resourceful laundress who undertook the stampede from Circle City. Mrs. Wills had gone north vowing to make a fortune to support her invalid husband. In Dawson, she staked a claim and then began cooking to finance her mining. She sold bread for a dollar a loaf until she had $250 in hand. With that, she purchased a single box of starch and opened a laundry.

Sometimes prospectors found travel easier in winter than in summer, because frozen rivers made it easier to pull sleds loaded with supplies. This team is hauling their load along Tomagon Creek in Alaska's Interior in November 1898. (Photo B89.24.16, Anchorage Museum)

Her laundry service paid for the labor to mine her claim. Mrs. Wills stubbornly resisted claim jumpers, and when her ground proved rich, she turned down an offer of a quarter-million dollars for her claim.

Klondike and/or Bust!

When the avalanche of humanity that roared through the Klondike was set into motion, there were but a handful of steamboats plying the mighty Yukon. There were four sizable sternwheelers plus another three or so smaller steamers serving the trading posts, settlements and mining camps.

The *Alice* was the first steamboat of the season into Dawson in June 1897, followed a day or two later by the *Portus B. Weare*. After off-loading liquor and food, and taking on gold and eager passengers, the two stern-wheelers slipped into the current and began the voyage downstream.

The steamers puffed down the muddy river for 1,700 miles, then another 60 miles along the Norton Sound coast. The *Alice* had left Dawson first but the larger *Weare* overtook her and arrived at St. Michael two days in the lead.

There was food at St. Mike, crates of tubers, bottles of cider, tins of apricots, cherries and pineapple. But the exultant kings and queens of the Klondike were still one step removed from civilization. After tasting the first fruits of their good fortune, they boarded waiting ocean steamers for the tedious, rolling voyage from the dreary outpost on Norton Sound to urban society and indulgence.

The NAT&T's *Portland* weighed anchor first, bound for Seattle, but the ACC's *Excelsior* was faster. It reached its home port of San Francisco three days ahead, on July 14, 1897.

The two treasure ships represented a tremendous storm front that broke upon the west coast of America

There's no glamour for J. Staley and his crew who are working the slopes of French Hill. Many gold-seekers paid far more for their northern escapade than they earned from any gold they found. (Courtesy of Pat Roppel)

and then rolled north. The statistics are eloquent. During the first five weeks of the stampede, 20 steamers left West Coast ports for Alaska. From Seattle alone, before the end of August, some 10,000 people and more than 36,000 tons of freight were swept north. Another 15,000 argonauts departed Puget Sound between January 1 and March 22, 1898. In February alone, there were more than 45 sailings from Seattle, and 41 ships based in San Francisco were reportedly operating on Alaska routes.

Steamship lines with established Alaska connections were of course among those to benefit from the frenzy. The San Francisco-based Pacific Coast Steamship Co. had long dominated routes to southeastern Alaska. Ships from San Francisco commonly called in Puget Sound or Victoria, B.C., en route to Alaska stops that included the district capital in Sitka and the mining town of Juneau, as well as Wrangell, Tongass, Glacier Bay and an assortment of Native villages, canneries and fishing ports. During summer, passengers included a fair number of tourists on Alaska excursions, by 1892, nearly 2,000 a year.

In western Alaska, shipping was dominated by the Alaska Commercial Co. Ships of the ACC supplied the company's string of trading posts, including posts on Kodiak Island, Dutch Harbor in the eastern Aleutians, St. Michael and the Yukon River camps and settlements.

Shortly before the Klondike gold rush, both the ACC and Pacific Coast Steamship faced fresh competition from Puget Sound interests. The ACC's rival was John J. Healy's North American Trading and Transportation. The company operated the *Portus B. Weare* on the Yukon and chartered vessels, notably the *Portland*, to carry supplies and passengers from Seattle to St. Michael, where they connected with the *Weare*.

Pacific Coast Steam's competition came first from an Oregon mariner, Capt. David Morgan. Morgan built a ship in Astoria for cannery work in Alaska in 1892, but soon added passenger accommodations. He undercut Pacific Coast's passenger fares to Southeast and began to attract travelers. Soon after that, a more serious challenge arose in the form of the Alaska Steamship Co.

Alaska Steam's explicit intent was to break Pacific Coast Steamship's grip on Southeast. The founding partners included Puget Sound steamboat men who complained that Pacific Coast carried freight from San Francisco to Alaska more cheaply than freight taken on in the Sound.

"We hope to revolutionize steamboating on the Alaska route," Alaska Steam partner George Lent announced. Seattle merchants and Northern Pacific Railroad officials were all for the Seattle-based upstart's attempt to capture the Alaska trade. Merchants and residents in Southeast also welcomed the competition.

Alaska Steam opened offices at Schwabacher's Wharf in Seattle, remodeled a modest wooden steamship, the SS *Willapa*, and began bi-weekly service to Alaska in March 1895. In quick response, Pacific Coast slashed fares. First-class fare from Seattle to Juneau plummeted from $52 to $20, and then to $12. Second-class tickets dropped from $30 to $6. The freight rate was around $3 a ton.

The Klondike stampede quickly trampled any competition among steamship lines. Overnight, for any ship headed north, at any fare, there were far more willing passengers than the ships could accommodate. Ships relegated to bone yards, some with dubious pasts, were patched up and pressed into service. The former yacht of an Indian rajah, a Cuban blockade-runner, an antiquated Chinese freighter were all part of the strange flotilla carrying argonauts toward the gold.

Ships were routinely overloaded to a perilous degree, and conditions aboard were often abominable. A passenger quoted by Berton described the Canadian steamer *Amur* as "a floating bedlam, pandemonium let loose, the Black Hole of Calcutta in an Arctic setting." The *Amur* had 500 passengers shoehorned into accommodations meant for 100. The dining room could comfortably seat only 26, so that meals took hours to serve. There were several hundred howling, yapping, miserable dogs in the hold.

Even worse, the *Clara Nevada* hauled dynamite, illegal on a passenger vessel. She exploded and sank between Skagway and Juneau, and everyone on board was lost.

One of the most fantastic voyages was made by a side-wheel steamboat dating from before the Civil War. The *Eliza Anderson*, built in Portland in 1859, was tied up in Seattle harbor when Klondike fever struck. The *Anderson* was serving as a floating roadhouse and

The various interests of Schwabacher Bros. placed the company in a good position to prosper during the gold rush. And they were one of the first businesses to see reaction to the rush firsthand when the Portland *steamed in to Schwabacher's dock in July 1897, carrying word of the Klondike strike. (Photo 143 by Boyd & Braas, Special Collections, University of Washington Libraries)*

This image shows an early view of the Bon Marché, which has grown into one of the largest department store chains in the Pacific Northwest. (Photo UW 5239, Special Collections, University of Washington Libraries)

gambling hall, but the ACC recommissioned her for a last run to St. Michael.

Making a top speed of 8 knots, the decrepit craft puffed into Kodiak harbor just ahead of a storm. Ignoring entreaties to wait out the gale, Capt. Tom Powers ordered the *Anderson* to cast off for Dutch Harbor. On the storm's second day, the coal supply ran out — some of the crew, it seems, had hidden half the coal sacks at Kodiak to ease their loading. The passengers' bunks were ripped apart and thrown into the furnace, followed by some wooden water tanks, the ship's furniture and the stateroom partitions. Miraculously, just when all seemed lost, a stranger clad in oilskins and rubber boots — a stowaway from Kodiak — seized the wheel and guided the desperate craft into a sheltered cove with an abandoned cannery. There was enough coal at the old cannery to get the *Anderson* to Unalaska. There, the ACC purser, over the strenuous objections of Capt. Powers, condemned the unhappy vessel. Twenty-eight passengers immediately booked passage for home, but the rest, their ardor for gold undimmed, chartered the whaling schooner *Baranof* to carry them the remaining 750 miles to St. Michael. At the venerable outpost, they transferred to riverboats bound for Dawson. They proceeded far enough up the Yukon that fall to get frozen in for the winter.

As outlandish as it was, the odyssey of the *Anderson*'s argonauts was not altogether unique. A similar fate befell the clients of erstwhile Seattle mayor W.D. Wood.

Acting swiftly at the start of the stampede, Wood, who was in San Francisco at the time, formed the Seattle and Yukon Trading Co. and chartered the *Humboldt*, a wooden propeller steamer. There were delays in organizing the ship's departure, the vessel was overbooked and crowded, and Wood narrowly escaped lynching when he attempted to sail without 25 tons of his passengers' personal baggage. The cargo was reloaded and the *Humboldt* finally left San Francisco on August 16, anchoring off St. Michael 13 days later.

Wood's clients had paid for through transportation to Dawson, but they found no riverboat waiting for them in St. Michael. There were only steamboat parts, fabricated in shipyards elsewhere and shipped to the beach at St. Mike. The stampeders unloaded the cargo, raised a tent community on the beach and set about helping to construct *Seattle No. 1*, the steamer on which they had all bought passage. Amid the discontent, Wood tried to slip away but he was forced to remain as a kind of hostage. The steamboat was completed in three weeks and raced up the Yukon chasing a smaller vessel, the *May West*, which had been finished one day earlier.

When the boats were about halfway to Dawson, the Yukon froze. The dogged stampeders threw up log cabins and settled in for the winter. Some named their community Woodworth, after Mayor Wood and the *May West*'s Capt. Worth. But most residents called it Suckerville. Wood was forced to part with supplies he had hoped to sell at a hefty profit in Dawson. He eventually fled Suckerville and made his way back to St. Michael on foot. After spring breakup, Wood's clients resumed their river journey. On June 25, 1898, they disembarked in Dawson, 314 days after setting sail from San Francisco.

Klondike author Pierre Berton estimates that 1,800 argonauts attempted the all-water route to Dawson in 1897. Only 43 made it, and 35 of those turned back because of the prospect of starvation in under-supplied Dawson. Including sourdoughs already in the country, there were some 2,500 stampeders frozen in along the Yukon below Dawson during the winter of 1897-98. On the headwater lakes above Dawson there were 30,000 more who had hauled their outfits through the mountain passes from Skagway and Dyea.

During the first winter of the Klondike stampede, there were still other thousands of argonauts working their way toward riches. Some of these were embarked upon all-American routes, striving to penetrate the coastal mountains of southcentral Alaska. Nearly 4,000 men and women set out to traverse Valdez Glacier. They ascended a series of steps in the glacial ice up a 20-mile slope to the summit gap in the Chugach Mountains. Some of the ice benches required block and tackle to raise goods. From the summit, the route descended for nine miles to alpine lakes and mountain streams that tumbled finally into the Copper River. Snow blindness, crevasses, avalanches, howling winds, blizzards and rain were among the hardships afflicting the Valdez argonauts. There were deaths on the trail and many turned back, but many crossed the ice during the spring of 1898. Few continued

Water wagons line up in downtown Dawson, where businesses ranged from photography studios to dressmaking shops and community baths. (Photo PCA 277-1-56, Alaska State Library)

on to the Klondike. Most prospected in Copper River country, where a number of sourdoughs were already mining modest claims.

The misery of the Valdez route was eclipsed by the horror of the route that led over Malaspina Glacier, a piedmont glacier sprawling more than 1,500 square miles near Yakutat Bay. Only a handful attempted this ill-chosen route. In the memoir of Arthur Dietz, who organized an expedition from the New York area, there are references to four parties totaling about 100 men. Dietz reports 41 deaths among the four parties, including his physician brother-in-law. Many more were permanently incapacitated by snow blindness, frostbite and other injuries.

Wonders Wrought by Gold:
Boom Towns, "Blue Rooms," Rails and Wheelmen

There were no easy routes to the gold fields, as everyone who set out for the Klondike found. But as the rush wore on, long-lasting changes were wrought that began to smooth the way.

Dawson was not the only boomtown produced by the Klondike gold rush. When the first stampeders steamed up Lynn Canal, the valley at the foot of White Pass was the site of a single homestead. The stampeders overwhelmed the homesteaders, set up a tent community and named their town Skagway. Within three months, there were 3,000 residents housed in 700 tents or wooden structures. There were three wharves, six lumber yards, 19 restaurants and 15 general stores. There were seven doctors, three dentists, two barbers, three laundries, six lawyers and a newspaper. In the fall of 1897, Soapy Smith arrived with a handful of cronies. They swiftly set up a crime syndicate, launching a host of gambling ventures, scams and schemes to skim money from the incoming horde.

Three miles northwest of Skagway, Dyea sprang up at the site of John J. Healy's old trading post at the foot of the Chilkoot Trail. There were 1,200 people in Dyea by mid-December 1897, and at least 4,000 by spring. There were stores and hotels, warehouses, a church, a school, a library and a newspaper. The *Dyea Press* wrote, pointedly, "Dyea has everything that every other town in Alaska has, except Soapy Smith."

One problem with both gateway settlements was the shallow water offshore. Into the breach sailed Capt. Elias W. Johnston, owner of Seattle Lighterage and Floating Dock Co. Early in the stampede, Johnston led a flotilla of boats, men and supplies from Puget Sound to Skagway. By March 1898, Johnston was installed in a spacious office in Skagway while overseeing construction of a

Abundant liquor and entertainment emporiums indicate that a rousing good time could be had in boomtown Dawson. This 1898 image of Front Street shows the Monte Carlo Theatre next door to the Horseshoe Saloon, which housed the Oatley Sisters' Concert and Dance Hall. The mother-daughter pair of Polly and Lottie Oatley gained success by singing ballads and dancing with miners. (Photo by Tappan Adney, reprinted from The Klondike Stampede of 1897-1898 *[1900])*

large warehouse in Dyea. He also directed the operations of at least nine lightering barges, loading and unloading ships too large to dock in the shallow harbors. Most cargo came ashore in Skagway, which had a dock built early on.

In May 1898, construction began on a narrow-gauge railway from Skagway over White Pass. The railroad was a boon to Johnston's business, bringing in ton after ton of freight. It secured Skagway's future, too, as the gateway to the interior. But for Dyea, it marked the beginning of the end. The feverish rush over Chilkoot Pass had abated. As the railway progressed inland, Dyea withered. In July 1898, Soapy Smith was killed and his gang was rousted, removing a last impediment to Skagway's development.

In February 1899, nine months after construction began, the first train rolled 22 miles to the top of White Pass with 100 jubilant guests. Five months later the line reached Lake Bennett. A year after that, crews working north from Lake Bennett and south from Whitehorse met at Caribou Crossing (now Carcross) to drive the last golden spike, on July 29, 1900.

The White Pass and Yukon Railway extended 110 miles, connecting the ocean port of Skagway with the upper limit of steamboat navigation on the Yukon, at Whitehorse. Four years after Carmack, Skookum Jim and Tagish (Dawson) Charley had found gold, just three years after the Klondike stampede began, it was possible to travel in comfort from Seattle to Dawson by ocean steamer, railroad and riverboat.

While thousands of laborers dug, filled, blasted and tunneled the White Pass railway into being, feverish developments were taking place at the other end of the Yukon transportation artery. A frenetic shipbuilding program was launched in the fall of 1897 on the beaches of St. Michael and in shipyards in Dutch Harbor, Seattle, Portland, San Francisco and elsewhere along the Pacific Coast.

The Canadian Pacific Railway diverted several vessels it was building for use on the Stikine River to the burgeoning Yukon trade. Wrecked or defunct ships were cannibalized for boilers, engines and fittings. Some boats were shipped in pieces from shipyards for assembly in St. Michael. Others were towed to Norton Sound intact or sailed under their own power. By spring of 1898, more than 60 boats and barges had been built or were under construction for the Yukon trade.

Three steamboats launched by the ACC during the 1898 season brought something new to Yukon travel: a touch of luxury. Built in Unalaska and towed to St. Michael, the *Susie*, *Sarah* and *Hannah* were named for the wives of three company officials. They were 222 feet long by 42 feet abeam. Sternwheelers of 1,130 tons, they could make 17 knots in slack water powered by 1,000-horsepower engines.

Each ship could accommodate 225 passengers in staterooms of two or three berths. Fresh linen and running water were novelties on the Yukon, where passengers on most vessels still drew river water with a bucket and rope. A "blue room" on the top passenger deck cosseted special guests with luxurious appointments. In the large dining rooms, trimmed in mahogany, uniformed stewards served meals on heavy silver service. "Thrashing their way up the river at night, ablaze with lights," writes Barry Anderson, "these new steamers brought a festive air to the Yukon."

The all-water route to the Klondike was considered the rich man's route, and it was costly by the day's standards. A first-class ticket from St. Michael to Dawson cost $90. The downstream fare was $65, because it took less time. First-class fare from St. Michael to San Francisco was $120. A first-class round trip between San Francisco and Dawson thus cost $395. It was a tidy sum at the turn of the century, though a pittance to the kings and queens of the Klondike.

More than 20,000 people passed through St. Michael during the summer of 1898. Tents sprouted along the muddy beach where a dozen steamboats were being built.

Warehouses, hotels, stores and saloons sprang up in town. To keep order, Army troops had founded Fort St. Michael in 1897, and additional troops sent the following year brought the local contingent to nearly 300. In 1899, the Army sent troops up the Yukon to garrison new posts at Tanana and Eagle City, near the Canadian border.

Across the border, the population of Dawson exploded during the summer of 1898. When the ice went out on Lake Bennett in May, the encampment ringing the Yukon's headwater lakes was set into clamorous motion. Within 48 hours, all the lakes were clear of ice and 30,000 men and women were bound headlong for the Klondike.

The flood of humanity was borne upon 7,124 vessels,

The first White Pass and Yukon Railway passenger train to leave Bennett carried $500,000 in gold dust. (Courtesy of Pat Roppel)

Klondike-bound gold-seekers wait at Lake Bennett for transportation down the lake and onto the Yukon River. (Courtesy of Pat Roppel)

carrying some 30 million pounds of food and gear. There were craft of all sizes, shapes and designs. There were rafts of logs, some with a lone sailor, others crowded with horses, oxen and dogs. There were Peterborough canoes that had been portaged over the passes. Among the flotilla were nine small steamboats, their boilers and fittings having been hauled over the mountains by animals and willful men. All but one of the little steamers made it through the swift water of Miles Canyon and the rapids called Whitehorse and Squaw. The five-mile reach

was so treacherous that Mounties stepped in and required women and children to walk around it. A wooden tramway was soon built to haul boats and outfits around the rapids for $25 a load.

The mass of goods that descended on Dawson quickly relieved a winter of deprivation. Low water in the Yukon Flats, near Fort Yukon, had obstructed riverboats at the close of the 1897 season. Some goods that had gotten through the flats had been waylaid in Circle, at gun point. The winter of 1897-98 had been grim in Dawson, even for those newly rich.

Now, during the summer of 1898, a parade of riverboats called at Dawson. The town was overrun. Thousands of argonauts swept in on the tide from Lake Bennett only to find that the Klondike's creeks had long since been thoroughly staked. Many simply continued downriver, barely stopping in the teeming beehive of Dawson. Others remained, hiring out to work other peoples' claims or lingering until rumors sent them stampeding to remote spots at the merest whisper of gold.

In 1899, the picture in the Klondike began to change again when major mining interests arrived. They bought up individual claims and barged in dredges and hydraulic mining equipment to reclaim gold with industrial means. Then with the discovery of gold on the beaches of Nome, Dawson's bubble burst. It was the Klondike stampede in reverse, half of the town's inhabitants rushing down the Yukon, jamming every available steamer, bound for the new El Dorado on the Bering Sea.

The peak of the Nome gold rush came during the summer of 1900. Decades earlier, gold colors had been found on the Seward Peninsula by members of the Russian American Telegraph Expedition, but it was not until the 1890s that prospectors had begun to make productive finds. In September 1898, a trio of prospectors struck gold on Anvil Creek, in the Snake River valley about 10 miles inland from Cape Nome. The creek turned out to be one of the richest gold-bearing streams ever found in Alaska. The Lucky Swedes, as the prospectors were known, although one was a Norwegian, incorporated the Nome Mining District with deliberately lax rules. They filed more than 40 claims in their own names and nearly 50 claims in the names of others, including local civil and military officials in a bid to secure their cooperation. The scheme infuriated later arrivals and might have erupted into considerable civil unrest had it not been for the discovery, in July 1899, of fine gold in the beach sand at the mouth of the Snake River.

Within days, some 2,000 men, women and children were shoveling beach sand into rockers wherever they could sink a spade. Claim jumping had been routine in the Nome district, given the dissatisfaction with how claims had been filed, but on the beach, no claims could be filed below the high tide line. A man or woman found an unoccupied spot and dug.

The richest sands were near the mouth of the Snake, but the golden beach was 50 to 200 feet wide and ran for more than 13 miles. Ruby-colored sands, generally 1 to 4 feet below the surface, produced the most gold, but ruby sand mixed with black volcanic sand yielded the stuff, too. The heavy yellow mineral was concentrated just above bedrock, which was 4 to 8 feet deep. A typical day's labor produced between $20 and $100 in gold dust. It was not fabulous wealth, but it was enough to make Nome, in the words of one Seattle newspaper, a "poor man's paradise."

Between $1 million and $2 million in gold was reclaimed from the beach of Nome in 1899, and a similar amount was recovered from a few dozen rich claims on area creeks. By fall, the population of the instant city topped 5,000. The town site was poorly drained and conditions were unsanitary, with sewage and waste often dumped into the Snake River, the main source of drinking water. Dysentery, pneumonia and typhoid fever were epidemic. Alfred Brooks, of the U.S. Geological Survey, nearly succumbed from typhoid contracted in Nome that fall. And the real rush was yet to come.

Food supplies were in question for the winter in Nome and a good many miners, satisfied with their take of a few thousand dollars from the beach, crowded aboard the last boats headed south for the winter. Their numbers were replaced that fall and winter by the influx of gold-seekers from within Alaska and Yukon Territory. Dawson began to empty in August and the exodus continued all winter. The frozen Yukon became a highway as stampeders mushed dog sleds, rode horse-drawn sleighs or walked, pulling sleds themselves. At least one man skated, averaging 40 miles a day where the ice permitted. The overland distance from Dawson to Nome was some 2,000 miles.

Then there were the "wheelmen," as bicyclists called themselves. The United States was in the grip of a bicycle craze at the turn of the century, and a good many "wheels" could be found in all the northern gold fields. At least one of the wheels in Nome had been ridden there from Dawson. During five weeks in February and March 1900, Ed Jesson had braved the mid-winter cold, the frozen Yukon and the windswept coast of Norton Sound to pedal from Dawson to Nome.

In 1900, Dawson was still an outlier of civilization but it was not as isolated as it had been, thanks to the newly completed White Pass railway. Nome, on the other hand, while easily reached during summer, was cut off in the winter by the frozen Bering Sea. Once the last ship sank below the southern horizon in October, there was no food, no medicine, no news in or out until June.

When Ed Jesson had mounted his wheel in Dawson that February, among his gear he had stuffed several

articles predicted that the rush to Nome might be bigger than the Klondike stampede of two years before.

Seattle to Nome:
Alaska's Wildest Gold Rush Town

When word of the golden beach sands of Nome began to spread across the continent, the resurgence in gold fever was eagerly fueled by newspapers, railroads and steamship lines.

"WOULD YOU LIKE TO BE A MILLIONAIRE?" asked the headline on one railroad advertisement. "Fortunes are made by men of nerve and decision who take advantage of opportunities.... Cape Nome is easily reached. No walking or packing. Steamers run DIRECT from SEATTLE to NOME CITY. The GREAT NORTHERN RAILWAY will take you to Seattle in two-and-one-half days, from St. Paul."

"Nome Gold," beckoned ads for John J. Healy's NAT&T Co. "Poor Man's Diggings, American Soil, 8 Days from Seattle." Already experienced in the Seattle to Norton Sound run, NAT&T claimed to offer "The Quickest Service — Cheapest in Price." Second-class steamship fare from Seattle to Nome cost just $60 to $70.

Seattle's population in the 1900 census was just more than 80,000, but by May of that year, an additional 20,000 argonauts crowded the city's streets and shops, awaiting the easy ride to riches. With time on their hands, and impaired by gold fever, the Nome-bound masses

copies of Seattle and San Francisco newspapers. Months old though they were when he rolled into Nome, the papers made him a popular man in town. Among the items of greatest interest were reports in the Seattle *Post-Intelligencer* that an invading army of argonauts was massing in that town and other West Coast ports. Estimates of gold-seekers who would set sail for Nome once the Bering Sea ice parted ran as high as 50,000 or even 100,000 people. Given the ease of reaching the coastal town and the allure of her golden beaches, the offered an inviting target for entrepreneurs, both legitimate and otherwise.

On sale was Nome clothing, Nome water filters and medicines, Nome stoves and tents. A.D. Palmer and Co. offered Palmer's Portable House, "Fire, Water, Wind and Frost Proof," with all the comforts of home. "A man well housed and comfortable...stands a much better chance of successfully extracting the treasure from the bosom of Mother Earth than one who shivers in a tent or an old shack," the company counseled.

To extract gold from beach sand, a wide variety of ingenious inventions was offered. According to gold-rush historian Terrence Cole, at least 35 different patented devices were for sale in Seattle. Yoho's Scientific Gold Trap was purported to be designed along "scientific principles," though it could be "operated by a boy." Reeve's Cape Nome Rocker weighed less than 40 pounds and cost $15. It was "Manufactured by a man who was mining on the Nome Beach last season and who has rocked out as high as $138 in twelve hours with a similar

machine." Conveniently, the rocker could be seen on exhibit inside a Palmer's Portable House erected on Columbia Dock.

The first steamships to head for Nome at the start of the 1900 season set sail in mid-April, well before the Bering Sea ice went out. The voyage was about 2,700 miles from San Francisco, 2,300 miles from Seattle. The early ships vied with one another seeking leads through the shifting ice pack. As their ships maneuvered to overtake rivals, argonauts lined the railings, cheering or jeering depending upon their relative progress.

The first ship to reach Nome anchored in the shallow water offshore on May 21. The steam whaler *Alexander* was followed by more than 50 steamships that season, bearing 15,000 to 20,000 people to Nome. During May and June, some 30 steamships sailed from Seattle alone,

By September 1900, the gold rush to Nome had come and gone. From the time of the initial discoveries in 1898 to fall two years later, thousands of people stomped the gold-laden beaches fronting Norton Sound and dug the benches inland from the shore where gold had settled in prehistoric beaches. About 15,000 people left Nome in fall 1900, leaving about 5,000 behind to contemplate the grandiose schemes that only recently had flowed freely down the streets of town. The Golden Gate Hotel represented some of these grand plans, but fire plagued the building. The hotel burned in 1901 but was rebuilt; in 1934 it burned again, and this time much of downtown Nome burned with it. (Photo B65.18.50, Anchorage Museum)

carrying about 11,000 passengers and tens of thousands of tons of freight.

Steamships great and small crossed the North Pacific bound for Nome, but not all the fleet was steam-powered. There were sailing ships as well, and many barges towed by steamers and tugs.

In essence, the armada that put to sea from West Coast ports in 1900 carried the city of Nome to Nome. "The ships that headed north," Terrence Cole writes, "carried knocked-down theaters, gambling halls, saloons, hotels, restaurants and everything else needed to construct an instant civilization on the shores of the Bering Sea."

On a single day, May 20, near the peak of the rush, four ships sailed from Seattle with 1,200 passengers and 5,000 tons of cargo. Some 12,000 people crowded the docks to see them off, according to Cole. Among the freight shipped that day was a newspaper printing plant, 30 tons of bar fixtures and liquor for a new saloon and "a complete banking outfit, including $200,000 in coin and currency" for the new Bank of Cape Nome. There were also rails and most of the gear for seven miles of narrow-gauge railway, 600 tons of coal, 300,000 feet of lumber and thousands of tons of general merchandise.

The beach in Nome was a scene of overwhelming chaos during the summer of 1900. The town site lacked a natural, deep-water harbor and ocean-going steamers were forced to anchor in the roadstead a mile or so from the coast. Passengers and cargo were transferred to shallow-draft barges and lightered ashore, or as close to shore as possible. The procedure usually left a few yards of water to be crossed. Most often, women were carried to terra firma on the backs of obliging men, while men leapt into the brine, shod in rubber boots or not.

The beach itself was a jumbled mass of baggage, freight and humanity, all deposited unceremoniously just out of reach of the waves. "It was almost impossible for anyone to locate his own freight or luggage," Cole writes. "Everything from pianos to sewing machines, bar fixtures and barrels of whiskey, was stacked along the beach, as well as huge shipments of lumber, grain, hay, general merchandise, mining machinery, hardware and food. Many of the boxes and crates were smashed open. A $10,000 shipment of canned goods broke apart, and all the labels washed off the cans." Unidentified cans were sold for 10¢ apiece.

The riotous conditions that greeted arriving "Nomads" resembled those that faced the early Klondike stampeders disembarking in Skagway and Dyea. And as at those boom towns, Capt. Elias Johnston soon turned up with the makings of a lighterage operation. The previous winter, Johnston had spent $54,000 assembling his equipment and supplies. In 1900 and 1901, he more than doubled his investment, returning $112,000 through lightering and handling freight.

Other entrepreneurs also found lucrative niches serving the miners. They opened stores and saloons, music halls, theaters, banks, newspapers, and medical, dental and law practices. The *Nome Nugget* was founded by pioneer journalist John F.A. Strong in 1901, and is still publishing. There were restaurants and hotels, including a number of floating establishments on ships that had borne argonauts to the golden sands.

One of the more unusual niches was found by Seattle businessman Charlie Ross. With the beach crawling with thousands of gold-seekers shoveling sand from virtually every available square foot, Ross observed that miners were touchy about where people relieved themselves. He built a series of outhouses that opened upon deposit of a quarter. The structures were placed so that the high tide flushed them out twice a day. In this way, Ross cleaned up.

Behind the beach and parallel to it, the town grew in a line. Early Nome consisted of Front Street and little

While some members of the northern community looked askance at some of the "entertainers" in their midst, the Ladies of the Line, such as Lucy Lovell, performed valuable services, grubstaking prospectors and miners, caring for the ill and contributing to community events. (Photo 277-1-187, Alaska State Library)

else. It was two blocks deep and five miles long. At the height of the rush, Nome was the most lawless town in America. With only a handful of deputy marshals and military police to keep the peace, roving gangs operated openly on the swarming streets.

Just as troubling was the official corruption, some of the most blatant in U.S. history. Powerful backroom politicians persuaded Congress to create a third judicial district in Alaska, to be based in Nome. Arthur E. Noyes was hand-picked as the new judge. When lawsuits were brought before him questioning the ownership of rich claims, Judge Noyes would place the claims in receivership and give each case lengthy consideration. Noyes appointed the receiver who operated the mine. That receiver, a crony named Alexander McKenzie, extracted gold to the benefit of the judge and his friends.

After the scheme had been in operation for some time, a group of outraged miners went to San Francisco to complain to the Circuit Court of Appeals. Noyes was ordered to desist but refused. He was ordered to appear before the court in San Francisco but refused. Two marshals were sent to arrest Noyes, the clerk of court and Alexander McKenzie. All three were found in contempt of court. But McKenzie was an influential political boss in the national Republican Party. After an appeal from President William McKinley, a Republican, Noyes' sentence was commuted and McKenzie's conviction was reversed. Only the clerk served time in jail. In Alaska,

Judge James Wickersham was dispatched from Eagle to clean up the court in Nome. He did so, as far as possible, before another political appointee replaced him.

Among the notables in Nome during the rush was writer Rex Beach, who wrote a best-selling novel, *The Spoilers*, based on the Noyes gang. Another familiar Nomad was Wyatt Earp, the former gunslinger and marshal of Tombstone, Ariz. Earp and a partner, C.E. Hoxie, kept the Dexter Saloon. At 52, the gunslinger had grown a bit thicker in the middle, but he was still not a man to be crossed. Earp had run a gambling house in Seattle before drifting north to Alaska, passing through

Rampart before moving on to Nome. Newspapers in Nome recount two occasions when Earp was arrested for interfering with marshals and military police who were quelling drunken brawls.

The stampede to Nome was even more meteoric than the rush to the Klondike had been. It peaked and passed in a single season. By September 1900, it was over.

The truth is that most of the beach gold had been harvested during the first few months after its discovery. During the summer of 1900, the frenetic toil on the beach produced $350,000 in gold, less than a third of the total mined during the previous year.

The lack of production was not from any want of effort. The army of argonauts worked and reworked the sand with a variety of contraptions. Many of them were ineffective despite being intricate and, as the *Nome News* described them, "wonderful to behold." Among the most amazing devices were monstrous beasts designed to mine the seafloor, dredges with long-necked suction hoses mounted on ungainly steel frames. One of these, dubbed the Red Elephant, was built on the beach at a cost of $30,000. The contrivance was operated in shallow water by a team of 15 men for several days, reportedly reclaiming 90¢ worth of gold, or 6¢ per crewman.

As in the Klondike, the hordes who moiled for gold on the beaches of Nome spent far more money than the value of gold they recovered. Miners on the beach in 1900, Terrence Cole writes, spent between $3 million and $6 million in their efforts to enrich themselves.

The free-for-all on the beach ended abruptly in the

FACING PAGE: *Elias W. Johnston (second from left) and Mrs. Johnston (second from right) show a party of Nome folks and visiting dignitaries a take from their Nome area claim. (Courtesy of Robert E. King)*

late summer of 1900. Several storms had struck during the summer but in early September, a series of blasts rolled in off the Bering Sea. Tides driven by winds reaching 75 mph on September 12 swept clean most of the beach and destroyed parts of the business district. Hundreds of miners lost everything in the storm and returned to the states aboard troop transport ships sent to evacuate them before winter. Several thousand people had come and gone from Nome during the summer; in the fall another 15,000 departed, leaving perhaps 5,000 residents. A half century passed before any city in Alaska again attained the size of Nome during its mad, golden summer.

The Rush Rolls On

While Nome's beach deposits excited the world, the real riches lay along the region's creeks. The Seward Peninsula produced $4 million to $5 million in gold each year from 1900 to 1905, mostly from the Nome district. Production was bumped higher in 1906 and 1907, when Nome's Third Beach Line yielded $15 million in two years. Alfred Brooks and Frank Schrader of the U.S. Geological Survey, the first geologists on the scene in 1899, had speculated that ancient beaches, shorelines formed when sea level had been relatively higher than today, could be as rich as the modern beach. Half a dozen of these raised beaches perhaps now lay buried beneath Nome's treeless tundra. Scant heed was paid the geologists's observation until two miners hit the pay streak of the Third Beach Line. The discovery spiked Alaska's gold production in 1906 to more than 1 million ounces, worth some $22 million. It remains the record year in Alaska for weight of gold produced.

Among the miners who cashed in on the creeks was Capt. Johnston, the lighterage magnate. As the rush passed and Nome began to settle down, Johnston withdrew from lightering and pursued a variety of business opportunities in the area. He was involved in the first abortive attempt to construct a harbor for the city, in 1905.

At about that time, a miner approached Johnston and asked to buy an old gasoline launch. The miner didn't have cash so Johnston traded for a mining claim, No. 8 Cooper Gulch. The claim had been unproductive, but the boat had been beached for a year and was in bad repair, so the deal appeared a fair exchange of items of marginal worth.

Appearances deceived. Johnston leased the claim to his father-in-law in the fall of 1905, and he promptly struck arguably the richest pay streak ever found in the Nome district. No. 8 Cooper Gulch became a tourist attraction in Nome, and by 1909 had yielded about $1 million in gold. Eventually, the claim produced nearly $2 million in gold.

Capt. Johnston repaired to a custom-built mansion on Seattle's Lake Washington in 1908. He became a pillar of the city's Arctic Club and helped bankroll an arts colony on Lake Washington, attracting among other intellectuals and artists Alaska's Sydney Laurence.

By the time of his death in 1928, a series of bad investments and costly lawsuits had depleted Capt. Johnston's fortune. The year after his death, a fire claimed his mansion and forced his widow, Maud, into modest circumstances. When she died in Seattle in 1963, at age 91, her sole mementos from Alaska were some photos returned by relatives and friends and a single necklace of gold nuggets mined from No. 8 Cooper Gulch.

Gold production on the Seward Peninsula declined after Nome's Third Beach was depleted, but mining and prospecting continued. Nome became a regional shipping and supply center and developed some desperately needed stability.

A Swedish immigrant who arrived in New York with $5 in 1887, John A. Nordstrom parlayed his Klondike earnings into the largest independent shoe store chain in the country. Nordstrom retired from the company that family members still run in 1928 and died in 1963. (Photo UW 17748, Special Collections, University of Washington Libraries)

This 1913 U.S. Geological Survey map shows the successive beaches that contained placer gold and spurred the rush to Nome. Initial discoveries were made inland on the creeks. The rush became a free-for-all when prospectors found that the current beach was laced with golden sands. Mining continued in the Nome area for decades after the rush peaked. Alaska Gold Co. still mines in the area as do a number of smaller operators. (U.S. Geological Survey Bulletin 533)

By 1904, telegraph links lessened the town's isolation. In the presidential election of 1900, when incumbent William McKinley had defeated William Jennings Bryan, the election took place on November 6, but no one in Nome knew the result until February 5, 1901. The news came in a newspaper delivered by mail over winter dog sled trails.

Work began on an Alaska telegraph system in 1900, at the height of the Nome stampede. The Washington-Alaska Military Cable and Telegraph System, known as WAMCATS, largely followed the Yukon River route reconnoitered by the Russian American Telegraph Expedition decades earlier.

Wireless telegraph stations connected Nome with St. Michael in 1901. Two years later, the two western towns were joined by wire with Tanana, Valdez and Eagle, and through an Eagle-to-Dawson line, with a Canadian telegraph system that reached Vancouver. By 1903, submarine cables linked Sitka, Juneau, Skagway and Haines. Finally in 1904, a submarine cable from Valdez through Sitka to Seattle joined WAMCATS with the rest of the United States. During the next two years, Seward, Wrangell and Ketchikan joined the system, and Cordova was added in 1909, knitting together most of Alaska's important towns.

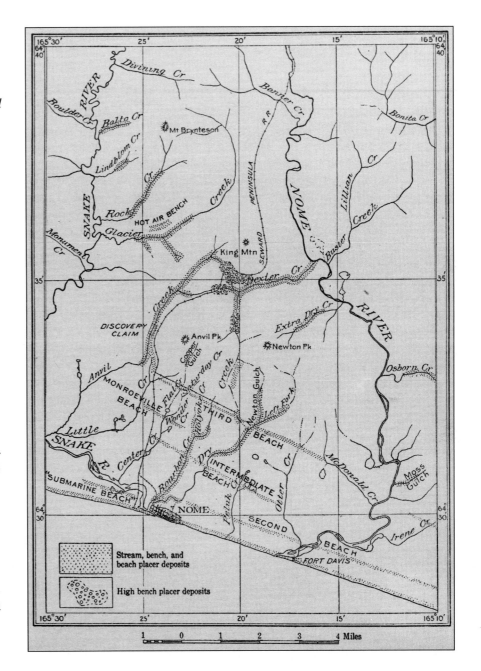

Gradually, wireless stations, easier to maintain, replaced the thousands of miles of land lines. Voice radio later diminished further the numbing isolation of Alaska's far-flung Bush. No longer would months pass before Alaskans felt the effects of world events. No longer would events in Alaska remain bottled up, awaiting breakup on the Yukon or the Bering Sea.

■ ■ ■

As the tide of argonauts receded from the golden beaches of Nome, it signaled the conclusion of one chapter in the Alaska gold rush story, but it was not the end. The next region to be touched by gold fever was the geographic heart of Alaska.

In 1901, trader E.T. Barnette hired a steamboat to carry a load of goods to the site of a proposed trading post at Tanacross, where the developing Valdez-to-Eagle Trail crossed the Tanana River. Army Capt. W.R. Abercrombie had blazed the route from Valdez part way in 1884 and all the way to the Yukon in 1898-99. Work was begun on a telegraph line from Valdez to Eagle in 1900, and it was apparent that the trail would become an important all-American route to Alaska's interior.

Barnette's steamer failed to reach the Valdez-Eagle Trail. Ascending the Yukon River some 700 miles, the *Lavelle Young* proceeded 300 miles up the Tanana to where Chena Slough enters from the north. The steamer turned into the slough in an effort to circumvent a maze of shallow channels ahead in the Tanana. The Chena was no improvement. The *Lavelle Young* was not of suitably shallow draft and was heavily laden. With Barnette and his wife were four employees, a dog team, a horse and 130 tons of supplies.

When the steamboat could navigate no farther, it tied up on the south bank of the Chena and off-loaded Barnette's party with their $20,000 worth of food, equip-ment and clothing. The event would later be celebrated as the founding of Fairbanks. But on August 26, 1901, no one was dancing on the banks of the Chena.

Barnette's stockpile of goods sat halfway up the Tanana to Tanacross, hundreds of miles short of the Valdez-Eagle Trail. There were no Indians evident and no mining nearby, although prospectors had probed the area off and on for a quarter-century. A pair of prospectors turned up almost immediately, however, lured by the *Lavelle Young*'s smoke, which they had seen from a nearby hill. One of the prospectors was an Italian immigrant, Felix Pedro. He assured Barnette that he and his partner had found colors in the area and hoped to make a strike soon.

Barnette began to fell logs for a trading post. He saw little alternative in any case. But the fur trade that winter turned out to be good, as Indians brought in marten skins. In March, Barnette and his wife took a dog sled loaded with fur to Valdez. They had not yet returned when Felix Pedro appeared at the trading post with news he had struck gold on a small creek a dozen miles from the post. It was late July 1902.

In September, Barnette persuaded a miner's meeting to name the already growing mining camp Fairbanks, after Sen. Charles Fairbanks of Indiana. The impetus came from Judge Wickersham, whom Barnette had met when the *Lavelle Young* was steaming upriver in 1901. Wickersham was heading downriver on his way to clean up Nome when his boat had tied up beside Barnette's at the mouth of the Tanana. He had asked the trader to name his yet-to-be-founded post for Fairbanks, who had helped secure the judge's appointment. Barnette saw the value of Wickersham's friendship. And indeed, when Wickersham later decided to move his courthouse to Fairbanks from Eagle, it helped legitimize the young stampede town.

Around Christmas, 1902, Barnette decided that the rush to Fairbanks that he anticipated needed a little push. He dispatched Japanese musher Jujiro Wada to Dawson to spread the word of Pedro's strike. Wada may have met Barnette as the cook aboard the *Lavelle Young*, but in any case, by 1902, Wada worked for the trader.

Wada's trip produced the hoped-for headlines in Dawson. "RICH STRIKE MADE IN THE TANANA," proclaimed the *Yukon Sun* of January 3, 1903. Hundreds of miners headed for Fairbanks that winter, only to find conditions were disappointing.

Jujiro Wada, right, figures prominently in several of Alaska's gold rushes. A man of remarkable stamina, Wada was sent by E.T. Barnette in 1902 from his trading post on the Chena River to Dawson City to spread word of Felix Pedro's strike in what would become the Fairbanks Mining District. Later the good citizens of Seward hired Wada and Alfred Lowell to scout the trail to the Iditarod mining area. In intervening years, Wada had become known for long-distance mushing exploits in Alaska and northwestern Canada. (Photo PA102560, National Archives of Canada)

Gold fields are not all alike and the placer gold of Fairbanks offered few easy pickings. There was gold to be had near the surface, and Felix Pedro had found some. But most of the stuff lay beneath 100 feet or more of overburden, much of it hard-to-excavate frozen gravel.

When the first stampeders descended on Fairbanks in early 1903, many creeks had already been staked by speculators exercising power of attorney for others.

The community of Solomon grew up near the mouth of the Solomon River when gold was found inland on the Seward Peninsula. (Alaska State Library)

There was little mining work to be had, too little food and no money. Some of the more hot-headed new arrivals blamed Wada for their predicament. Only his fleet feet enabled the musher to escape lynching. Wada outlived the wrath of his accusers and went on to become a legendary musher in Alaska.

Gold production in Fairbanks in 1903 was an unimpressive $40,000, but it jumped to $600,000 the next year and reached $6 million in 1905. The record year of gold production in Alaska was 1906, when the Fairbanks district contributed 40 percent of the total, or 400,000 ounces of gold, worth $9 million.

Although slow to start, the Fairbanks district turned

out to be the richest gold district in Alaska, producing more than 8 million ounces, fully a quarter of the state's production to date. It produced more than the Juneau district, twice as much as Nome and more than Circle, Fortymile, Innoko, Iditarod, Council and Solomon, Chichagof, Livengood, Willow-Hatcher Pass, Valdez and the Kenai Peninsula combined. Only the Klondike's total production exceeds that of Fairbanks, and after 1905, annual production of the Fairbanks district outpaced the Klondike every year.

Because it took time and money to develop gold mines around Fairbanks, the town did not explode the way Dawson, Circle or Nome had done. All the same, within five years, Fairbanks grew into a modern town. It had electric lights, a water system and a volunteer fire department. There were stores and hotels, schools and churches, a hospital and several newspapers. It had a telephone system that extended to outlying mining camps and communities. The Tanana Valley Railroad, with just four flatcars for rolling stock, ran from Fairbanks to Chena and beyond to neighboring mining camps. Both prospecting and active mines were widespread throughout the surrounding area and Fairbanks became the supply center for interior Alaska.

The growth of Fairbanks spurred development of a trail to Valdez. Roadhouses sprang up at convenient intervals along the route, which became known as the Richardson Highway.

The expansion of settlements in interior Alaska was one of several forces after the turn of the century that began to affect commerce on the Yukon River. The growth of Fairbanks and Chena drew Yukon riverboats up the Tanana River and established the village of Tanana as a major port and transfer point for cargo. Mining camps sprang up seemingly everywhere, and dozens of individual operators and small steamboat companies

began to run steamers up any tributary deep enough to float a boat. The big navigation companies, even ACC and NAT&T, struggled to make a profit in the face of their many smaller competitors.

In 1901, the ACC merged with two other transportation companies, then split off a pair of related firms. Northern Navigation Co. ran riverboats while Northern Commercial Co. operated the network of trading posts. Northern Commercial stores, direct descendants of Russian American Co. posts, still serve Bush communities today, on the eve of yet another century.

Another development in 1901 soon reshaped river commerce. The White Pass and Yukon Railway bought into the steamboat business. White Pass purchased the fleet of a Whitehorse-based navigation company as well as the winter stage line between Whitehorse and Dawson. The White Pass subsidiary, British Yukon Navigation, operated warehouses, a shipyard and winter storage facilities for vessels in Whitehorse. The shipyard produced new steamboats for the BYN fleet and, with railroad connections to Skagway, the company was able to dominate commerce on the upper Yukon. BYN delivered freight on the upper Yukon more cheaply than shippers coming through St. Michael were able to do. The balance of traffic on the great river began to shift from one end to the other.

In 1913, a rate war erupted between Northern Navigation and a White Pass subsidiary set up to compete within Alaska. White Pass slashed its through freight rates from Seattle to Chena from $45 to $25 a ton. In spring of 1914, Northern Navigation gave up. The company sold everything to the Canadians: 42 steamboats, 54 barges and all its facilities along the Yukon and its tributaries. The triumph didn't last long. An independent American riverboatman, George Black, soon stepped in to compete with the Canadians, beginning

on the smaller streams. His firm prospered and survived the winds of change on the Yukon for nearly 40 years.

■ ■ ■

As the first decade of the 20th century unfolded in Alaska, miners and prospectors were scattered widely across the landscape. Gold was sought everywhere and was found in many places, usually in small but tantalizing amounts. Dozens of mining camps sprouted along the upper Yukon, flourished, then faded, soon to be reclaimed by the taiga and the shifting riverbeds. Hardy prospectors pursued gold along the Koyukuk River, pushing deep into the Brooks Range.

Gold was found on the Yentna River in 1905, and sourdoughs soon spilled through passes in the Alaska

Nome wasn't the only gold camp on the Seward Peninsula. Solomon, Council, Bluff, Candle and a host of others lured prospectors. If gold in sufficient quantities was found, miners worked the ground. As technology improved and more money was available, small mining operations consolidated and sometimes were taken over by mining conglomerates. This group of workers is building a ditch to redirect water for mining operations in the Solomon River valley east of Nome. (Alaska State Library)

Range, into the Kuskokwim drainage. In 1906, the yellow metal was found on the headwaters of the Kuskokwim, and the following year, a strike on a tributary of the Innoko River spurred a rush to McGrath.

Gold fever was soon epidemic in other areas of Alaska. Seward, on the Kenai Peninsula, aggressively promoted itself as the gateway to new gold fields in the western Interior. Seward itself had been founded in 1903 by a group of Seattle-based businessmen who saw the ice-free port on Resurrection Bay as the logical terminus for a railroad to Alaska's interior. Among the organizers of the Alaska Central Railway was company vice president John McGraw, the former Washington governor who had been among the first Klondike stampeders. A series of loosely connected trails linked Seward with McGrath and Ophir, both in the Innoko district, and onward to Kaltag, on the lower Yukon. From Kaltag, an overland mail trail led to Nome. The trail system from Seward to Iditarod to Nome eventually achieved fame as the Iditarod Trail.

In the spring of 1908, the Alaska Road Commission hired a party to survey the trail from Seward to Kaltag. They followed the Alaska Central Railway bed for 54 miles to Turnagain Pass, then traveled around Turnagain Arm and over Crow Pass to Eagle River. From there, they crossed Knik Arm and ascended the Yentna, Skwentna and Happy rivers to Rainy Pass. They descended a series of rivers in the Kuskokwim drainage to the vicinity of McGrath, crossed overland to Ophir, then to Dishkaket and finally to the Yukon River just below Kaltag.

The survey took nearly two months to complete. It concluded the route offered good winter travel to Iditarod and Nome and was 400 miles shorter than the alternate route from Valdez by way of Fairbanks.

The mounting gold fever stimulated by the Yentna and Innoko finds was overwhelmed by the discovery of a rich pay streak on Otter Creek, an Iditarod River tributary. The strike came on Christmas Day, 1908, and within a year, there were more than 1,000 people in the district, concentrated in the villages of Iditarod and Flat.

Iditarod was soon being called "another Klondike," and stampeders were rushing in not only from within Alaska but from outside. When a Valdez booster mounted

Before miners can tell exactly how pure their gold is, the metal has to be melted down and analyzed at an assay office, such as this one at Iditarod. (Courtesy of Pat Roppel)

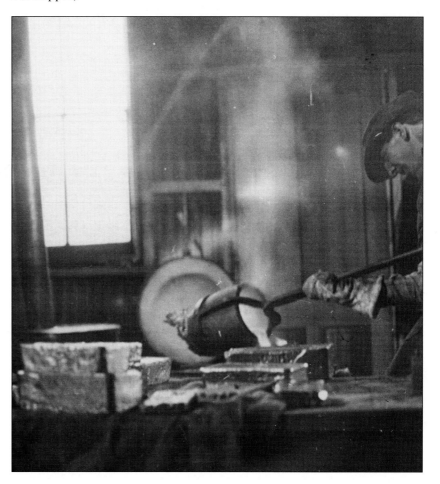

One of the results of the lust for gold was the development of transportation and communication systems more suited to the expanding population and commerce of the gold rush. Two mules pulled the first tram-passenger coach at Iditarod in August 1911. (Courtesy of Pat Roppel)

a campaign to publicize the Valdez-Fairbanks-Iditarod trail, Seward businessmen formed the Seward Commercial Club to promote their own town as the logical jumping-off point for the newest diggings.

First, the club published a pamphlet, *Seward, The*

Iditarod-Alaska

Gateway to the Iditarod! Next, they decided stampeders needed a descriptive log of the trail, based on the most reliable accounts. They dispatched Jujiro Wada, the musher who had stirred up the Fairbanks stampede, and Alfred Lowell, whose family had homesteaded Resurrection Bay before the railroad entrepreneurs arrived. In the years since the Fairbanks stampede, Wada had achieved widespread fame and respect for his exploits in the Arctic. In addition to describing the trail to Iditarod, the pair were to blaze and mark the trail where necessary, and scout sites for roadhouses along the way.

Wada and Lowell set out in early December 1909. On January 25, they reached Dishkaket and returned a report to Seward on their investigations. They estimated the distance to the gold fields at around 550 miles from Seward. The mushers had broken and staked about 25 miles of trail, shortening the route by about 20 miles. They reported on the cabins and roadhouses already along the trail.

The pair described the trail as mostly good, except for four miles of the Happy River that were subject to overflows and avalanche-prone Indian Pass, on the way to Eagle River. They also described the gold fields: On the Innoko tributary of Yankee Creek, 100 miners were working a pay streak 100 feet wide. Along Otter Creek, where the Iditarod strike had been made, 600 holes had been sunk, and all that had reached bedrock showed pay dirt. In addition, coarse gold had been found on Ophir Creek and nearby Ganes Creek.

Wada and Lowell returned to Seward on February 26, 1910. Even as they made their way back, the *Portland* was on its way from Seattle carrying the first stampeders of the year to Seward. When Wada reached the port town, he quickly set sail for Seattle, announcing that he would pick up a group of gold-seekers and personally guide them to Iditarod.

Among the stampeders who traveled the Seward-Iditarod Trail in early 1910 was George A. Terrill, a 60-year old sourdough who had lost both his legs to frostbite in the Tanana district. Terrill traveled the winter trail to Iditarod on a pair of wooden legs.

The 1910 census found 1,200 people in Iditarod that spring, twice the number of people in Seward. By summer, the Iditarod district had at least quadrupled in population, and it was estimated that 4,000 people would remain during the winter.

Maj. Wilds Richardson of the Alaska Road Commission spoke in Seward in June. He supported trail improvements but lacked the funds to initiate work. The commission's top priority was the Valdez-Fairbanks Trail, and funds were inadequate even for that. Nevertheless, the commission marked the Seward-Iditarod Trail that winter. They also blazed and repaired parts of the trail, both from Iditarod and from the end of the railway, then at mile 72 from Seward. Travel time from Iditarod to Seward was about three weeks under good conditions. In late December, the first shipment of gold arrived in Seward, a half-ton of gold dust, driven down Fourth Avenue with much celebration.

In 1911, Congress appropriated $150,000 for the Seward-Iditarod Trail. Even as the trail was improved, work on the railroad ground to a halt. Lacking a world-class mineral deposit such as had made the Copper River railroad profitable, railroad construction in Alaska was too expensive to be privately funded.

Seward held on until the federal government jumped into the railroad construction business, but the boom in Iditarod soon began to fade. More than $2 million in gold eventually came out of the Iditarod and Innoko districts, and the craze over Alaska gold had not quite run its course. But for most Alaskans, as the second decade of the century wore on, fever for gold had broken. ◼

LEGACY OF GOLD

The stampedes to reclaim Alaska's gold were crucial events in the region's history, but they fell far short of transforming the great land into a fully modern state. Alaska was too big, too rugged to be so easily subdued, the population was too sparse, the climate too intemperate, the land altogether too wild.

Before the gold, Alaska had been but a dim and distant possession of the United States. After the rush, Americans at least knew where it was and were more familiar with its unique problems. Despite this enlightenment, Alaskans were entrusted with a degree of self-determination only by small steps.

The issue of home rule for Alaska had been raised in Congress beginning in 1881. A far-reaching bill in the 47th Congress would have empowered a territorial governor and established a court system and a legislative council. It would have extended public land laws and provided for the collection of local taxes and for the election of a non-voting delegate to Congress. The Senate Committee on Territories approved the bill. But the 47th Congress adjourned in 1883 without debating, much less voting on the bill.

In 1884, the First Organic Act gave limited power to a handful of appointed civil authorities in Alaska, but further progress toward self-determination was slow in coming. Not until Alaska gold seized the nation's attention in 1897 did Congress gradually begin to take note of its vast northern holding.

From the first rumblings in 1881, winning a share of local control over Alaska affairs was a process that took years:

• 19 years before Congress permitted limited taxation to support local development and enacted a code of civil and criminal law specifically for Alaska, in 1900;

• 22 years before laws providing for the survey and

FACING PAGE: *Shorey's Old Book Store, shown here when it was located in the Occidental Hotel Building at the corner of Third and Cherry in downtown Seattle, was among the Seattle businesses that profited from the gold rush. (Photo 1109, Museum of History and Industry)*

Among the legacies of the northern gold rushes was increased interest in Alaska. Alaska had been treated haphazardly by the United States government after it purchased the territory from the Russians in 1867. This meant that some government services readily provided elsewhere could not be had in Alaska. Not until 1912 did Alaska become an official Territory with its own Senate, and House of Representatives, shown here. For the first time, Alaskans were able to enact legislation. (Photo PCA 01-2178, Alaska State Library)

sale of public lands were fully extended to Alaska, in 1903;

• 25 years before Alaskans were granted a non-voting delegate to the House of Representatives, in 1906;

• 31 years before Alaska officially became a United States Territory and a legislature was formed, in 1912; even then, Congress retained the power to overrule any enacted legislation, to regulate fish, game and fur, and to approve the governor, who was still not popularly elected.

Another 47 years passed before Alaska became a state, in 1959, 92 years after the United States bought Russian America.

To achieve these steps, it was not only bureaucratic inertia that had to be overcome, although that was a factor, particularly in the days before the gold rush. A larger problem was that, in essence, Alaska was an American colony. It had a colonial relationship with the federal government. It had a classic colonial economy in which outside interests exploited natural resources and siphoned away the profits.

The salmon and fur industries were controlled by investors in California and Washington state. So were the steamship lines. As mining developed, it was increasingly dominated by nationally prominent corporate concerns that bought up individual claims and mined not with rockers and gold pans but with hydraulic gear and dredges operated by wage workers.

Investors outside Alaska were by and large opposed to Alaska home rule. They were generally satisfied with the arms-length style of government practiced in Washington, D.C. And in any event, their money could often buy influence in the nation's capital when it was needed. In their minds, Alaska home rule spelled less control and higher taxes.

The group that came to personify such "outside interests" to most Alaskans was the Alaska Syndicate, formed in 1906 by the Guggenheim brothers and J.P.

Morgan. The Syndicate leaped into Alaska with the $3 million purchase of the Kennecott copper mines, in the Chitina Valley. In 1907, the group took over the railroad already begun up the Copper River valley from Cordova. They spent $20 million to complete the 211-mile Copper River and Northwestern Railroad. The staggering investment was more than returned during the quarter-century the world-class copper mines were worked.

Nor were the Syndicate's interests confined to copper. The Guggs, as the Alaska Syndicate came to be known, also acquired a controlling interest in the parent company of Alaska Steamship. The company's steamers carried general merchandise to Alaska and copper ore on the return voyage south. The Guggs bought a dozen canneries to add to their Alaska investments, representing about an eighth of the Alaska salmon pack.

The struggle in Alaska between corporate interests on the one hand and trust-busting reformers on the other reflected a larger national preoccupation. In Washington, the energetic former judge James Wickersham, elected in 1908 as Alaska's non-voting delegate to the U.S. House, vigorously opposed the Guggenheim interests and promoted Alaska home rule. It was a draining, uphill fight.

Following the frantic influx of people and spending that constituted the gold rush, Alaska's population and economy leveled off. The 1910 census showed 64,356 people in Alaska, just 764 more than the 1900 census. During the next decade, people left the territory. Alaska's 1920 population dropped 15 percent, to 55,036.

Despite the declining population, development in Alaska pressed on. Roads were continually upgraded. The Alaska Railroad made its way north to Nenana, the new port town on the Tanana, and to Fairbanks. The U.S. Geological Survey, which had begun work in Alaska before the gold rush, established a separate Alaska Division in 1903. The division's chief, Alfred Brooks, deposits and systematically surveyed and mapped topography and geology across vast reaches of Alaska. Between 1889 and 1924, USGS geologists and topographers mounted spectacular expeditions penetrating hundreds of miles of little-known country in the Yukon, Kuskokwim, Copper and Matanuska drainages, and in the Alaska Range and the Brooks Range, traveling by horse, sled dog, boat and foot. USGS maps and reports aided not only stampeders and mining engineers but road and railroad construction. Here, at least, was tangible federal work in support of opening Alaska.

■ ■ ■

The changes wrought by northern gold were not confined to Alaska. The years of the Klondike and Nome stampedes and their aftermath were decisive for Seattle as well.

At the start of the Klondike stampede, Robert Moran was an established ship builder, a former mayor and business leader in Seattle. It was Moran Bros. shipyard that patched together the aging *Eliza Anderson* for Alaska Commercial Co. before her ill-fated voyage to Unalaska in 1897.

Between January and June of 1898, Moran Bros. shipyard turned out a dozen steamboats for the Yukon River trade, along with an even larger number of barges. On June 28, the riverboats sailed for St. Michael, with Robert Moran commanding the fleet. When it was time to leave the sheltered Inside Passage of the Panhandle and set out across the Gulf of Alaska in the shallow-draft boats, two of the boats' captains had second thoughts and Moran had them put ashore. One boat was lost on the dangerous crossing, but the entire crew was rescued. The other 11 boats went into service on the Yukon in August, some seven months after their keels were laid.

Moran's exploit enhanced an already sound reputation

As daring in person as his company was industrious in boat-building, Robert Moran led a fleet of Moran-built steamboats north from Seattle to St. Michael near the mouth of the Yukon. All of the crews and all but one of the boats survived the trip across the gulf and up the west coast of Alaska. (Photo 1961, Museum of History and Industry)

had mapped in the Yukon-Tanana Uplands during Dawson's boom summer of 1898, and in the Nome area the following year, during the first months of that town's great commotion. Survey scientists were in all the gold fields, sometimes before the rush.

The USGS studied gold, coal and other mineral

and he emerged from the gold rush with one of the largest shipyards in the United States. In 1902, Moran Bros. began building the battleship USS *Nebraska*, a project that took two years to complete. The shipyard was sold in 1906 and later became Seattle Construction and Dry Dock Co. By 1914, there were 26 shipbuilding firms in Seattle, employing more than 5,000 workers.

A number of companies prominent in Seattle today proudly trace their lineage back to the gold rush. The first Bon Marché department store opened in Seattle in 1890, established by a German immigrant named Edward Nordhoff. As a young man, Nordhoff had worked in a

The Rainier Brewery, in business at least since 1886, stood ready to help slake the thirst of any passing gold-seeker. (Photo 83.10.6078.1, Museum of History and Industry)

Paris department store, where he became enamored of a rival store acclaimed for its service and integrity, the Maison à Boucieaut au Bon Marché. Nordhoff emigrated to the United States in 1881 and moved to Seattle in 1890, where he and his wife Josephine invested their savings of $1,200 in a small dry goods store that they called Bon Marché.

One of Nordhoff's retailing innovations was his use of pennies. At the time, pennies were scarce on the West Coast and merchants made change to the nearest nickel. On his first buying trip East, Nordhoff returned with sacks of pennies, which he used to support "economy sales" with advertised prices like 19¢. Through such innovations and much hard work, the Nordhoffs survived the Panic of '93 and held on until the boom of the Klondike rocked Seattle in 1897. The Bon Marché thrived on the gold rush trade, despite Edward's death in 1899. Josephine, a 27-year-old mother of three, took the reins and managed the store's expansion in 1900, and the purchase of Cooper & Levy, Pioneer Outfitters, in 1901.

Josephine Nordhoff died of cancer in 1920, at age 48, a respected, even beloved civic figure in Seattle. Her original store was replaced in 1929 by a $5 million store at the Bon Marché's present downtown site. It was sold the same year to a chain of retail establishments. In 1992, the parent company of Bon Marché was reorganized under Chapter 11 bankruptcy and emerged as a public company operating more than 220 stores in

26 states with annual sales exceeding $7 billion.

The success of the retail enterprise founded by John Nordstrom was based more directly on the gold rush. Nordstrom's partnership in a Seattle shoe store was financed by gold he mined in the Klondike.

Nordstrom arrived in New York in the 1880s with $5 in his pocket, a Swedish immigrant who spoke not a word of English. He worked his way west as a miner, logger and longshoreman before heading north to the Klondike from Seattle in 1897. Nordstrom returned to Seattle in 1899 with $13,000 in gold. He invested some of his money in real estate and, in 1901, opened a shoe store with a partner.

Wallin & Nordstrom shoe store started business slowly. In 1929, Wallin sold out to his partner and a year later, John Nordstrom sold the business to his three sons. Thirty years later, the family had 27 stores, representing the largest independent chain of shoe stores west of the Mississippi. In 1963, the brothers purchased Best Apparel fashion stores in downtown Seattle and in Portland, concentrating their upscale business on high quality and service. By the early 1980s, a third generation continued expansion of the Nordstrom chain, opening stores in Alaska, Washington, Oregon, California and Utah, with annual gross sales of $500 million.

Clinton C. Filson's story is a tale of success on a more modest, more personal scale. Filson was born in Ohio in 1850, homesteaded in Nebraska and worked as a railroad conductor before settling in Seattle in 1897. Along the way, he had also operated a small store outfitting loggers. He tapped this experience in opening Filson's Pioneer Alaska Clothing and Blanket Manufacturer, specifically targeting Klondike stampeders. Filson operated his own mill, manufacturing heavy-duty clothing, blankets, sleeping bags and foot-gear designed for the Yukon. Everything was manufactured by the Filson Unit-Garment

Method, in which each piece was made completely by a single worker, rather than assembled in pieces by an assembly line process. Filson also kept in contact with customers and refined his goods to meet their needs.

After the gold rush, Filson expanded his business targeting loggers as well as miners. He patented a successful jacket in 1914, the Filson Cruiser, and became established as one of the premier makers of quality outdoor clothing in the Pacific Northwest. Filson died in 1919, but his company retains both his name and his reputation for uncompromising quality.

The list of contemporary Seattle businesses with gold rush roots is long. A partial list compiled by the Klondike Gold Rush Centennial Committee of Washington State identifies nearly three dozen concerns, from C & G Cigar Store, to Shorey Books, Pacific Northwest Bell, several banks, a boiler works and an iron works, from the Carnation Co. of evaporated milk fame to Rainier and Olympia breweries. Virtually any business in existence in Seattle during the gold rush received a boost. And while the push was nearly universal in Seattle, it was important in some economic sectors in other West Coast cities as well, from San Francisco north to Vancouver, B.C.

■   ■   ■

In Alaska, the gold rush era closed just prior to World War I. As a result of the rush, the population had doubled and was dispersed broadly throughout the land. Trails dotted with roadhouses took travelers from Valdez to Fairbanks, from Seward to Iditarod and Nome. The White Pass and Yukon Railway carried people and freight from Skagway to the riverboat terminus in Whitehorse. And on the mighty Yukon itself, dozens of boats bore freight and passengers from mining camp to mining camp, from village to village.

Telegraph links kept villages informed. Deputy

FACING PAGE: By the end of the 20th century, Nordstrom has become a renowned apparel merchandising chain. The business began during the Klondike gold rush when John Nordstrom took some of the $13,000 in gold he brought back from the Klondike and, with a partner, opened a shoe store in Seattle. (Photo 1758, Special Collections, University of Washington Libraries)

marshals and judges kept the peace as best they could. The Alaska Railroad was under construction as were coal mines in the rail belt. Government scientists probed the wilderness and produced maps and reports for public use. Corporate interests were fully involved in the Territory's affairs, to the alarm of some citizens. But there was an elected delegate in the U.S. House of Representatives who could make the case of the people, although he was not always heard.

The shape of Alaska on the eve of the 21st century owes itself to many things: to the discovery of oil at Prudhoe Bay, to statehood, to the Second World War that both opened road access to the rest of the continent and catapulted Alaska into the air age. But before any of these came the gold rush.

The legacy of Alaska's gold was change. The glint of gold in the Far North triggered an upheavel that moved Alaska materially closer to Seattle and to the rest of the country. The gold-seekers a century ago blazed trails, founded settlements, forged economic ties and, through feats of strength, persistence and daring, helped to fill the void on the map where most of Alaska had until then resided.

The argonauts' tales of the Klondike, Nome and other northern gold fields also filled a void in the American imagination. In that imaginative space, Alaska's gold rush lives today. ■

FROM GOLD FIELDS TO POOR HOUSE

BY R.N. DeARMOND

Editor's note: *A lifelong Alaskan and eminent historian, Bob was born in Sitka in 1911 and currently resides with his wife, Dale, in the Sitka Pioneers' Home.*

On Aug. 16, 1896, a U.S. Navy deserter named George Carmack and his two Indian companions picked up some gold nuggets in what became known as Bonanza Creek in northwestern Canada. That triggered a stampede to the site from the mining camps of Fortymile and Circle City and when the news reached Seattle and San Francisco in July 1897, the Klondike gold rush began. A second rush to the North began two years later with discovery of gold near Cape Nome.

It has been estimated that at least a hundred thousand people journeyed to the Northland during that heady gold rush era. Most of them had high hopes of getting rich, but few had any real idea of how to go about it. A reporter of the Klondike scene, "Stroller" White wrote that aboard the ship that brought him north there were two lines of thought. One held that a man would do best if he worked alone, holding a sack with one hand and shoveling gold with the other. The other line favored two-man teams, with one man holding the sack while the other scooped in the nuggets.

Alaska's non-Native population increased from 4,298 in 1890 to 30,493 in 1900 and most of the increase was undoubtedly after 1896. What do we know about those people, mostly men, who came to Alaska in those years seeking their fortunes? What, to use the technical term, were the demographics? Where were they born? What were their ages? Were they married or single? Did they have children? If they had a trade or profession, what was it?

We do know something about some of the people who came north during the gold rush and then left again. There was Key Pittman, who went from Nome to Nevada and became a U.S. senator from that state. Wilson Mizner gained fame as a raconteur. Clarence Berry turned his interest from gold to California oil and became a multimillionaire. Jack London and Rex Beach flourished as writers. Kate Rockwell kept right on being Klondike Kate, and so on.

FACING PAGE: *Former Marine Corps buildings were refurbished and converted to the first Pioneers' Home in Sitka. This image shows the Home as it appeared in 1924. (Courtesy of Candy Waugaman)*

There is, however, a group of little-known men, and a few women, about whom some specific information is available. These were people who had stayed on after the glory days were past. They had become Alaskans and had toiled at earning a livelihood for themselves and, for some, their families. They had varying success, but in the end because of age, ill health, improvidence or just plain bad luck, they were no longer able to care for themselves.

By 1912, the year the Territory of Alaska was created by Congress, the problem of caring for indigent leftovers from the gold rushes was being considered in several quarters. At Fairbanks, Igloo No. 4 of the Pioneers of Alaska had proposed building a home for the care of elderly prospectors. They had not, however, found a way to fund such an institution. And at Sitka in 1912 a U.S. Marine Corps barracks was abandoned and its

Pioneer Home Buildings, Sitka Alaska 4/24
The Photo Shop Studio

Sitka Pioneers' Home resident Andrew Morrison came to the Klondike prospecting for gold in 1897. A native Canadian from Prince Edward Island, Morrison sought his fortune first in Dyea, then in the Yukon Territory, Circle City, Nome and Council. He entered the Pioneers' Home in 1921 and remained there until his death in 1932. (Courtesy of R.N. DeArmond)

buildings were standing empty. A few Sitka people proposed that the buildings be converted to a home for pioneer prospectors. Again, funding was the problem.

Funding for both proposals became a possibility after the First Territorial Legislature convened at Juneau in March 1913. The legislators were sympathetic to the cause. Eighteen of the 23 members of the House and Senate had come north during or before the gold rushes. Eleven of them were directly engaged in some phase of gold mining.

Rep. Dan Driscoll of Fairbanks introduced the first bill. It created the awkwardly titled "Board of Prospectors Home Commission" with the governor, the secretary of Alaska and the delegate in Congress from Alaska as board members. They were to select a site and provide for a suitable building. The bill quickly passed both houses and was signed into law by Gov. Walter Clark. There was an appropriation of $6,000 to acquire a site and put up a building, and $5,000 to run the place for a year. But the bill had one serious flaw. It directed that the site would be "at one of the several hot springs of Interior Alaska."

There were, unfortunately, "several" hot springs and all of them wanted the facility. The board members were unable to agree on a site, the building was never erected and the law was repealed in 1923.

Sitka almost didn't get a Pioneers' Home that year either. Permission had to be received from the Navy Department in Washington D.C. for the use of the Sitka buildings, and that did not arrive until the 60-day session was almost at an end. But a bill was rushed through and signed into law. It appropriated $10,000 and created the Alaska Pioneers' Home at Sitka, to be governed by a board of three trustees. The trustees were the governor and two public members appointed by the governor.

The law provided that "(e)very worthy pioneer, or other person, who shall have been a resident of the Territory of Alaska for five years preceding his application for admission and who shall need the aid or benefit of said Home in consequence of physical disability or other cause within the scope of the regulations of the board, shall be entitled to admission thereto subject to the conditions, limitations and penalties prescribed by the rules and regulations of the board."

The old Marine Corps buildings were repaired and refurbished, mostly by volunteers. The Alaska Pioneers' Home was dedicated by Alaska's new governor, John F.A. Strong, on July 4, 1913, and it opened for business on Sept. 2. It was often referred to as the Poor House, but the five applicants for admission who were waiting on the doorstep ignored that. All were admitted and by year's end, the number of residents had reached 34. At the end of a full year of operation the facility was nearing its capacity and additional applications were being received.

With the Sitka Pioneers' Home nearly full and the Fairbanks area facility still unbuilt, the 1915 legislature erected an additional safety net for needy Alaskans. This act provided a cash "allowance," as it was called, for individuals 65 or older who had lived at least 10 years in Alaska. The maximum allowance was $12.50 a month, paid quarterly. Subsequent sessions of the legislature lowered the entry age for women to 60 years and doubled the monthly allowance they could receive. The allowance was gradually raised, during the years the program was in effect, to a maximum of $30 for men, $60 for women. The funds were a part of the Pioneers' Home appropriation and the program was administered by the Board of Trustees of the Home.

The Sitka Pioneers' Home received its first residents on Sept. 2, 1913. On July 14, 1961, it admitted the last man who can be certainly identified as a gold rusher. He was Edward Louis Crawford, a native of New York state, who had come north in 1896 and was at Fortymile when George Carmack displayed his Klondike gold at Fort Cudahy in August 1896.

A total of 933 men and women who came north in the years 1896 to 1900 applied between 1913 and 1961 for admission to the Sitka Home or to the assistance program administered through the Home. There were far more men than women among those 933, and since women were not admitted to the Home until 1950, their applications were for financial assistance.

The Prospector, a 13 1/2-foot clay and bronze statue, has been a fixture in front of the Sitka Pioneers' Home since 1949. Sculptor Victor Alonzo Lewis modeled the statue after a true pioneer, William "Skagway Bill" Fonda. (Staff)

The questions asked on the application forms included date and place of birth, date entered Alaska, whether a U.S. citizen, trade or occupation, names of parents and other relatives and "where did you live and work in Alaska?"

The information that follows is derived from those applications.

The people in this group were not youngsters when they came north. The largest age group among the 933 were people in their 30s, 360 of them. There were 274 people in their 40s when they began the grand adventure, and only 185 in their 20s. There were 71 in their 50s, 36 were under 20 and 7 were in their 60s.

They were a motley crew, so far as their birthplaces were concerned. The foreign-born slightly outnumbered American-born, 473 to 450. Ten did not record place of birth on their applications. The Scandinavian countries contributed heavily: 86 from Sweden, 77 from Norway and eight from Denmark. There were also 22 who had been born in Finland. The British Isles produced 84 gold-seekers and Canada another 83. Of the former lot, 47 were from Ireland, 23 from England, 12 from Scotland and two from Wales. There were 58 from Germany, 12 from Austria, eight from Italy, seven from France and four from Switzerland.

The USS Pinta *is moored in Sitka Sound in this photo of Sitka in the 1890s, at the beginning of the Klondike gold rush. (Courtesy of R.N. DeArmond)*

The rest are from widely scattered countries. There were three each from Yugoslavia, Greece and New Zealand; two each from Australia, Estonia and Alsace-Lorraine, and one each from Armenia, Luxembourg, Japan, the Philippines, Poland, Portugal, Russia, Turkey and Uruguay.

A great majority of the foreign-born, however, had come to the United States from five to 25 years before the Klondike discovery. Many had become citizens or had at least received their first papers. Unfortunately, the applications do not indicate where they were living when the gold bug overtook them. The same is true for the native-born. They also had a variety of backgrounds, with birthplaces in 38 of the then 45 states and the District of Columbia, but none in the three territories.

Somewhat surprisingly, the greatest number, 54, were born in New York state. Next in order were Wisconsin 36, Pennsylvania 35, Michigan 33, Illinois 30, Massachusetts 29, Maine 24, Iowa and California each 23, Ohio 22, Missouri and Minnesota each 12, Oregon 11, Maryland and Indiana each 10, Kentucky 9, Texas 8; Washington and Vermont each 7; New Jersey, Tennessee and

Virginia each 5; West Virginia, North Carolina and Montana each 4; Georgia, Nevada, Colorado, Connecticut, New Hampshire and Louisiana each 3; Alabama, Mississippi and District of Columbia each 2; and South Dakota, Florida, Rhode Island and Kansas 1 each.

In the early years, 1896 to 1899, the target for most of the gold-seekers was Circle City or Dawson City and most of them went in by way of Dyea or Skagway. Some of them didn't get there at once. And some never did reach the gold fields. John Baker, a native of Norway, reached Juneau in 1896 and worked for a year to earn the money for the outfit required for entry into Canada. Then he went on to Dawson, mined there for two years and followed the stampede to Nome where he mined and worked as a laborer for 27 years before entering the Pioneers' Home.

John Bjornson, born in Sweden and a resident of the United States since 1882, was headed for Dawson when he landed in Skagway in 1898. But he got a job on the new White Pass railway and stayed with it until he left for Sitka in 1935.

Even those who got to Dawson usually remained there for only a few years. They went on to Nome, or to one of the many new mining districts that were being opened. On the whole, the men who went to Dawson seem to have been a restless bunch and moved around a good deal, and they wound up in camps large and small in all parts of Alaska.

It was different with those who first went to Nome. It was a lot easier to get there than it was to Dawson, and many who went to Nome

spent their entire working careers on the Seward Peninsula.

The big permanent camps such as Fairbanks and Nome sent the greatest number of men to the Pioneers' Home at Sitka, but nearly every camp in Alaska was represented: Ruby, Ophir, Iditarod, Circle City, Rampart, Wiseman, Berry, McCarthy, Flat, Chicken, etc.

The original law contained no minimum age requirement for admission to the Pioneers' Home. Ten men entered while still in their 40s. The youngest was only 42, and he lived in the home for 30 years until his death in 1947. Fifty-five men were admitted while in their 50s, and 91 entrants were 60 to 64. The largest number, 213, were aged 65 to 69; 203 were 70 to 74 and 161 were 75 to 79. Men in their 80s when they entered the home numbered 151; 23 were in their 90s.

The oldest of the gold-rush-era men to enter the Pioneers' Home was Peter Wilson at 95 years and 10 months. That was on Feb. 28, 1957. Wilson was born in Solverborg, Sweden, in April 1861. His father was Swen Olson and, following an ancient Scandinavian custom, the son became Peter Swenson. In 1891, he landed at San Francisco from a sailing ship and soon moved up the coast to Astoria and became a fisherman. He was somewhat late in catching the Klondike fever and did not head for Dawson until the spring of 1899. He had enough of the gold fields after a few months and moved to Ketchikan where he resumed fishing. He became a naturalized citizen of the United States on

May 18, 1921, taking the name Peter Wilson in the process. He never married and continued fishing until in his 80s when he retired to live alone in a small cabin. His savings ran out in 1956, and from then until he entered the Pioneers' Home he had received a small grant from the Territorial Department of Public Welfare. That agency had been created in 1937 and had taken over the assistance grants program from the Pioneers' Home Board of Trustees. Wilson died on Jan. 9, 1958, and occupies Grave No. 1346 in the Pioneers' Home Cemetery at Sitka.

Within the limits of a tight budget, the Pioneers' Home provided sanctuary for men who were destitute. They were given shelter, a bed, three meals a day, laundry service, clothing as needed and tobacco, not cigarettes or smoking tobacco, just plug chewing tobacco. A physician was in attendance from the beginning, but many of the men were in worse physical condition than had been expected and a nursing staff was soon added.

One thing the home could not provide was privacy. Some of the wards had 20 or more beds and the beds were close together. Most of the gold rush men had lived alone for years, with hours to suit only themselves. The lack of privacy was probably the major reason that 158 men, after having entered the Pioneers' Home, left again of their own free will. One man arrived on a steamer, made a quick tour of the home and got back aboard the steamer. A few others stayed only a few weeks or months, but for the most part the ones who left did so after a year or more. They had received some medical attention and got the wrinkles out of their bellies and were ready to strike out again on their own.

Fifty-nine of the 158 men who left the home later returned. Some of them left and returned several times. The other 99 who left did not return. Some went to live with relatives in the Lower 48. Many of them, having recovered their health, applied for and received an allowance under that program and went back to living as they had before.

Nine men were discharged by the management. "Insobriety and insubordination," "continual drunkenness" and "fighting and insubordination" were the stated reasons. Seventeen of the gold-rush era residents became demented, were turned over to the federal authorities and sent to the sanitarium at Morningside near Portland, Ore.

One of the problems of the Home management was keeping the able-bodied residents corralled. They were used to the outdoors and some of them had tramped over half of Alaska, prospecting for gold. It was a habit they did not give up easily, but this was unfamiliar country and they frequently got lost. Most of them were soon found and returned, but the remains of others were not discovered for weeks or months.

One wanderer was John Lauchart, a native of Austria who had come to the United States in 1872 and to Dawson in 1897. He had also spent time at Nome and at several other camps before entering the Home in October 1929. He left the Home at 4 a.m. on May 27,

1930, and disappeared. Following a three-day search, a reward of $25 was offered for his return. Tom Haley found him on June 7 near the head of Silver Bay, a dozen miles from town. "He was returned to town in fair condition for having been 10 days without food," the report stated.

In making this study, the material and family status of only 350 of the gold-rush era men was tabulated. Of these, 189 had never married, according to the statements on their applications. Another 89 were widowed, 47 had been married but were divorced or separated, and there were doubts about some of the 25 who wrote "Married" on their applications. One man added, "but don't know where she lives," and another, "Married, but haven't seen her in years."

To the question, "Do you have children," 90 of the men answered, "Yes." A few had children in Alaska, but the majority had not seen their children since they came to Alaska and many had not recently heard from them. "Have one son and two daughters but don't know where they are," one man wrote. Another wrote, "I haven't heard from any of my relatives in 30 years." But some of the men had kept in touch with relatives and when their addresses were recorded they were duly notified by Home management of the demise of the resident.

There were more than just a few women who came north in the gold rush era, but as the women's Pioneers' Home did not open until 1950, when they found themselves in need they applied for financial assistance under the

allowance program. Most of them had been widows and had been supporting themselves for some years before they applied for assistance.

Margaret Ann Dates, born in Cayuga, N.Y., in 1852, was 46 when she landed in Skagway with her husband. From there they went to Eagle and Circle, where her husband died. She moved to Fairbanks and then to Valdez where she did dressmaking and hair dressing, ran a bath house and a rooming house. In 1919 she was granted an allowance of $12.50 a month, later raised to $20.

One of the women who never married was Katherine Schneider, a native of Germany, who was 54 when she landed in Juneau in May 1898. That fall she moved to Skagway and in 1901 she went to Valdez, where she stayed. She taught music and languages, but she spent part of each year 1909-17 in Bellingham, Wash., because she did not have enough pupils in Valdez to make a living. In September 1920 she was granted $25 a month from the Territory. She was 76 by then and she lived for only a few additional months.

A great majority of the 923 men and women who applied for assistance from the Territory of Alaska when they reached old age had earned an honest living, paid their bills and been good citizens. Six of the men had had sufficient standing among their peers that they were elected to serve in the Territorial Legislature. As provided in the original Act in 1913, "every worthy pioneer" had been welcomed to the safe haven of the original Alaska Pioneers' Home. ∎

BIBLIOGRAPHY

Anderson, Barry C. *Lifeline to the Yukon: A History of Yukon River Navigation*. Seattle: Superior Publishing Co., 1983.

Barry, Mary J. *Seward Alaska: A History of the Gateway City, Vol. I: Prehistory to 1914*. Anchorage: M.J.P. Barry, 1986.

Berton, Pierre. *Before the Gold Rush*. Toronto: McClelland and Stewart, Inc., 1993.

—. *Klondike: The Last Great Gold Rush, 1896-1899* . Toronto: McClelland and Stewart, Inc. 1972.

Cole, Terrence. *Nome, City of the Golden Beaches*. Alaska Geographic, Vol. 11, No. 1. Anchorage: Alaska Geographic Society, 1984.

—. *Wheels on Ice: Bicycling In Alaska 1898-1908*. Anchorage: Alaska Northwest Publishing Co. 1985.

Dawson City. Alaska Geographic, Vol. 15, No. 2. Anchorage: Alaska Geographic Society, 1988.

Dietz, Arthur Arnold. *Mad Rush for Gold In Frozen North*. Los Angeles: Times-Mirror Printing and Binding House, 1914.

Dorpat, Paul. *Seattle Now and Then*. Seattle: Tartu Publications, 1984.

Eagle-Fort Egbert: A Remnant of the Past. Fairbanks: U.S. Bureau of Land Management, 1989.

Fairbanks. Alaska Geographic, Vol. 22, No. 1. Anchorage: Alaska Geographic Society, 1995.

Gates, Michael. *Gold At Fortymile Creek: Early Days In The Yukon*. Vancouver: University of British Columbia Press, 1994.

Graburn, Nelson H.H., Molly Lee and Jean-Loup Rousselot. *Catalogue Raisonne of the Alaska Commercial Company Collection*. Berkeley: University of California Press, 1996.

Gruening, Ernest. *The State of Alaska*. New York: Random House, 1968.

Holeski, Carolyn Jean and Marlene Conger Holeski. *In Search of Gold, The Alaska Journals of Horace S. Conger 1898-1899*. Anchorage: Alaska Geographic Society, 1983.

King, Robert E. "Captain Elias W. Johnston, Gold Rush Transportation Businessman." *Alaska History*, Vol. 11, No. 1. Anchorage: Alaska Historical Society, 1996.

McDonald, Lucile. *Alaska Steam, A Pictorial History of the Alaska Steamship Company*, Vol. 11, No. 4. Anchorage: Alaska Geographic Society, 1984.

Minter, Roy. *The White Pass, Gateway to the Klondike*. Fairbanks: University of Alaska Press, 1987.

Morgan, Murray. *Skid Row: An Informal Portrait of Seattle*. Seattle: University of Washington Press, 1982.

Neufeld, David and Frank Norris. *Chilkoot Trail, Heritage Route to the Klondike*. Whitehorse, Y.T.: Lost Moose, The Yukon Publishers, 1996.

Nichols, Jeannette Paddock. "Advertising and the Klondike," *The Washington Historical Quarterly*, Vol. 13, No. 1. January 1922.

Sale, Roger. *Seattle: Past to Present*. Seattle: University of Washington Press, 1976.

The Sea Chest, Vol. 20, No. 3. Seattle: Puget Sound Maritime Historical Society, March 1987.

Sherwood, Morgan B. *Exploration of Alaska, 1865-1900*. Fairbanks: University of Alaska, 1992.

—. *Alaska and Its History*. Seattle: University of Washington Press, 1967.

Skagway, A Legacy of Gold. Alaska Geographic, Vol. 19, No. 1. Anchorage: Alaska Geographic Society, 1992.

Speidel, William C. *Sons of the Profits, or There's No Business Like Grow Business! The Seattle Story, 1851-1901*. Seattle: Nettle Creek Publishing Co., 1967.

Wharton, David. *The Alaska Gold Rush*. Bloomington: Indiana University Press, 1972. ■

INDEX

A.D. Palmer and Co. 61

Abercrombie, Capt. W.R. 68

Adney, Tappan 15

Alaska Central Railway 20, 73

Alaska Commercial Co. 16, 18, 21, 32, 35, 36, 40, 41, 45, 47, 50, 71

Alaska Gold Co. 67

Alaska Mining and Milling Co. 40

Alaska Steamship Co. 50

Alaska Syndicate 79

Alaska-Yukon-Pacific Exposition 36, 37

Alexander 61

Alice 16, 17, 47-49

American Bank of Alaska 2

Amur 50

Anderson, Barry C. 40, 43

Anvil Creek 33, 58

Arctic 45

Arctic Circle 36

Arctic Club 81

Argonauts 4

Ash, Harry 48

Astoria 50

Australia 27

Baker, John 91

Baranof 53

Barnett, E.T. 68, 69

Beach, Rex 11, 63, 86

Beardslee, Capt. L.A. 43

Bella 47

Berry, Clarence 86

Berton, Pierre 16, 33, 47, 48, 53

Birch Creek 47

Bjornson, John 91

Black, George 71

Bon Marché 52, 81, 83

Bonanza Creek 12, 15

Brainerd, Erastus 10, 25, 26, 32, 33, 36, 37

British Yukon Navigation 71

Brooks, Alfred 59, 65, 79

Canadian Pacific Railroad 23

Carmack, George Washington 12, 15, 32, 47, 48, 86

Charley, Dawson (Tagish) 12, 15

Chilkoot Pass 28, 38

Chilkoot Trail 28, 29, 43

Chilkoots 43

Choquette, Buck 33

Circle City 47

Clara Nevada 50

Clark, Gov. Walter 88

Cole, Terrence 61, 62, 65

Commodore 40

Constantine, Charles 47

Cooper & Levy 25, 29, 30, 83

Cooper Gulch 2

Crawford, Edward Louis 89

Cudahy, Michael 47

Dates, Margaret Ann 92

Dawson 2, 4, 16, 32, 54, 55, 57-59

Dawson, George M. 16

Dearmond, R.N. 86

Decker Bro's. General Merchandise 24

Dietz, Arthur 27, 54

Douglas Island 10

Driscoll, Dan 88

Dyea 55

Earp, Wyatt 63

Eckberg, Scott 30

Edmonton 21, 33

Eldorado Creek 15

Eliza Anderson 51, 53, 80

Elliott Bay 4

Emanuel, Richard P. 2

Etholin, Lt. Adolph K. 18

Excelsior 18, 33, 49

Fairbanks 33, 68, 70, 71, 87

Fairbanks, Sen. Charles 68

Filson, Clinton C. 60, 83, 84

First Organic Act 7, 76

First Territorial Legislature 88

Fischer Bros. 25

Fonda, William 89

Fort Cudahy 17

Fort Reliance 41

Fort Selkirk 43

Fort St. Michael 57

Fortymile River 15, 45

French Hill 49

Gerstle, Lewis 35

Glenora 33

Gold, physical properties of 4

Golden Gate Hotel 61

Gruening, Ernest 7

Gustison, Allen 10

Haley, Tom 92

Hannah 56

Harper's Weekly 15

Harper, Arthur 18, 41, 44

Harris, Richard 35

Healy, John Jerome 47, 50, 55

Hegg, Eric A. 44

Holt, George 41, 43

Horseshoe Saloon 55

Hoxie, C.E. 63

Hudson, N.E. "Teddy" 45

Humboldt 53

Iditarod 2, 34, 73-75

Iditarod Trail 73

Indian River 15

Innoko 34

Jenkins, William D. 26

Jesson, Ed 59

Johnston, Capt. Elias W. 2, 55, 62, 65, 66

Johnston, Maud (Mrs. Elias W.) 65, 66

Juneau 10, 21, 24, 33

Juneau, Joe 35

Klondike Kate 86

Klondike River 4, 15

Ladue, Joe 15, 16, 27

Lake Bennett 58

Lauchart, John 92

Laurence, Sydney 66

Lavelle Young 68

Lent, George 50

Lewis, Victor Alonzo 89

Lippy, Tom and Salome 18, 31

Livengood Camp 45

Livengood, Jay 45

London, Jack 11, 86

Lovell, Lucy 63

Lowell, Alfred 69, 75

Lucky Swedes 59

MacDougall and Southwick 25

Malaspina Glacier 54

Mason, Skookum Jim 12, 15

May West 53

Mayo, Al 18, 41, 44

McGrath 72

McGraw, John 20, 25, 73

McKenzie, Alexander 63

McKinley, Pres. William 63

McQuesten, Jack 18, 41, 44, 47, 48

Mercier, Francois 18

Mexico 4

Mizner, Wilson 86

Monarch 2

Monte Carlo Theatre 55

Moran Bros. 25, 30, 31, 80, 81

Moran, Robert 80

Morgan J.P. 79

Morgan, Capt. David 50

Morgan, Murray 36

Morrison, Andrew 88

Nebraska 81

New Racket 43-45
Niebaum, Gustave 35
No. 8 Cooper Gulch 66
Nome 4, 7, 33, 59, 62, 63, 65-67
Nome Mining District 59
Nordhoff, Edward 11, 81, 83
Nordhoff, Josephine Patricia McDermott 11, 83
Nordstrom, John A. 66, 83
North American Trading and Transportation Co. 16, 47, 50, 60, 71
North West Mounted Police 28, 38, 47
Northern Commercial Co. 71
Northern Navigation Co. 71
Northern Pacific Railroad 50
Noyes, Arthur E. 63

Oatley Sisters' Concert and Dance Hall 55
Oatley, Lottie 55
Oatley, Polly 55
Ogilvie, William 17, 47
Olmsted, Frederick Law 36
Olson, Swen 91

Pacific Coast Steamship Co. 50
Panic of 1893 25, 30, 83
Pedro, Felix 68, 70
Pinta 90

Pioneer Square 8
Pittman, Key 86
Portland 12, 18-20, 25, 29, 32, 33, 49-51, 75
Portland 23, 33
Portland-Alaska Outfitting Co. 23
Portus B. Weare 16, 18, 47, 49, 50
Powers, Capt. Tom 53

Rabbit Creek 12
Rainier Brewery 81
Rampart 43
Raymond, Capt. Charles P. 40
Richardson Highway 71
Richardson, Maj. Wilds 75
Rockwell, Kate 86
Ross, Charlie 62
Ruby 42
Russian American Co. 21, 40, 71
Russian American Telegraph Expedition 58

San Francisco 4, 20, 21, 32
Sarah 56
Schieffelin, Ed 41, 43
Schneider, Katherine 92
Schrader, Frank 65
Schwabacher Bros. 25, 51
Sea Lion 19
Seattle 4, 8, 10, 20, 24, 27, 35, 36, 76, 84
Seattle and Yukon Trading Co. 20, 53

Seattle Construction and Dry Dock Co. 81
Seattle Hardware 25
Seattle No. 1 53
Service, Robert 11
Seward 74, 75
Seward Commercial Club 74
Shorey's Old Book Store 76
Sitka 7, 86, 88-90
Sitka Pioneers' Home 86-92
Skagway 10, 54, 55
Sloss, Louis 35
Smith, Soapy 54
Snake River 59
Solomon 70
Spiedel, William 23
St. Michael 12, 16-19, 49, 56
St. Michael 41
Staley, J. 49
Steele, Samuel B. 47
Stewart River 44
Stone, Charles 32, 33.
Strong, John F.A. 62, 88
Stuart, E.A. 30
Suckerville 53
Susie 56

Tacoma 8, 23
Taft, William Howard 36
Tanana Valley 4, 33
Tanana Valley Railroad 71
Tebenkov, Lt. Michael D. 18
Telegraph system 67
Terrill, George A. 75
The State of Alaska 7

Third Beach Line 65, 66
Tlingits 43
Tolovana River 45
Tomagon Creek 48
Tombstone 43
Trans-Alaska Gopher Co. 29
Treadwell Mine 10, 40
Treadwell, John 40

University of Washington 36, 37

Valdez Route 54

Wada, Jujiro 69, 70, 75
Wallin & Nordstrom 83, 85
Washington-Alaska Military Cable and Telegraph System 67
Weare, Portus B. 47
West Coast Connection 6, 8
Western Fur and Trading Co. 41
White Pass and Yukon Railway 10, 33, 56, 57, 71
White Pass Trail 28, 29
Whitehorse 10
Wickersham, Judge James 63, 68
Willapa 50
Wilson, Peter 91
Wilson, Sen. John 32
Wood, Col. W.D. 20, 53
Woodworth 53

Yukon 7, 40, 41, 44
Yukon River 4, 10, 38, 44

ALASKA GEOGRAPHIC. Back Issues

The North Slope, Vol. 1, No. 1. Out of print.

One Man's Wilderness, Vol. 1, No. 2. Out of print.

Admiralty...Island in Contention, Vol. 1, No. 3. $19.95.

Fisheries of the North Pacific, Vol. 1, No. 4. Out of print.

Alaska-Yukon Wild Flowers, Vol. 2, No. 1. Out of print.

Richard Harrington's Yukon, Vol. 2, No. 2. Out of print.

Prince William Sound, Vol. 2, No. 3. Out of print.

Yakutat: The Turbulent Crescent, Vol. 2, No. 4. Out of print.

Glacier Bay: Old Ice, New Land, Vol. 3, No. 1. Out of print.

The Land: Eye of the Storm, Vol. 3, No. 2. Out of print.

Richard Harrington's Antarctic, Vol. 3, No. 3. $19.95.

The Silver Years, Vol. 3, No. 4. $19.95.

Alaska's Volcanoes, Vol. 4, No. 1. Out of print.

The Brooks Range, Vol. 4, No. 2. Out of print.

Kodiak: Island of Change, Vol. 4, No. 3. Out of print.

Wilderness Proposals, Vol. 4, No. 4. Out of print.

Cook Inlet Country, Vol. 5, No. 1. Out of print.

Southeast: Alaska's Panhandle, Vol. 5, No. 2. Out of print.

Bristol Bay Basin, Vol. 5, No. 3. Out of print.

Alaska Whales and Whaling, Vol. 5, No. 4. $19.95.

Yukon-Kuskokwim Delta, Vol. 6, No. 1. Out of print.

Aurora Borealis, Vol. 6, No. 2. $19.95.

Alaska's Native People, Vol. 6, No. 3. $24.95. Out of print.

The Stikine River, Vol. 6, No. 4. $19.95.

Alaska's Great Interior, Vol. 7, No. 1. $19.95.

Photographic Geography of Alaska, Vol. 7, No. 2. Out of print.

The Aleutians, Vol. 7, No. 3. Out of print.

Klondike Lost, Vol. 7, No. 4. Out of print.

Wrangell-Saint Elias, Vol. 8, No. 1. Out of print.

Alaska Mammals, Vol. 8, No. 2. Out of print.

The Kotzebue Basin, Vol. 8, No. 3. Out of print.

Alaska National Interest Lands, Vol. 8, No. 4. $19.95.

Alaska's Glaciers, Vol. 9, No. 1. Revised 1993. $19.95.

Sitka and Its Ocean/Island World, Vol. 9, No. 2. Out of print.

Islands of the Seals: The Pribilofs, Vol. 9, No. 3. $19.95.

Alaska's Oil/Gas & Minerals Industry, Vol. 9, No. 4. $19.95.

Adventure Roads North, Vol. 10, No. 1. $19.95.

Anchorage and the Cook Inlet Basin, Vol. 10, No. 2. $19.95.

Alaska's Salmon Fisheries, Vol. 10, No. 3. $19.95.

Up the Koyukuk, Vol. 10, No. 4. $19.95.

Nome: City of the Golden Beaches, Vol. 11, No. 1. $19.95.

Alaska's Farms and Gardens, Vol. 11, No. 2. $19.95.

Chilkat River Valley, Vol. 11, No. 3. $19.95.

Alaska Steam, Vol. 11, No. 4. $19.95.

Northwest Territories, Vol. 12, No. 1. $19.95.

Alaska's Forest Resources, Vol. 12, No. 2. $19.95.

Alaska Native Arts and Crafts, Vol. 12, No. 3. $24.95.

Our Arctic Year, Vol. 12, No. 4. $19.95.

Where Mountains Meet the Sea, Vol. 13, No. 1. $19.95.

Backcountry Alaska, Vol. 13, No. 2. $19.95.

British Columbia's Coast, Vol. 13, No. 3. $19.95.

Lake Clark/Lake Iliamna, Vol. 13, No. 4. Out of print.

Dogs of the North, Vol. 14, No. 1. $19.95.

South/Southeast Alaska, Vol. 14, No. 2. Out of print.

Alaska's Seward Peninsula, Vol. 14, No. 3. $19.95.

The Upper Yukon Basin, Vol. 14, No. 4. $19.95.

Glacier Bay: Icy Wilderness, Vol. 15, No. 1. Out of print.

Dawson City, Vol. 15, No. 2. $19.95.

Denali, Vol. 15, No. 3. $19.95.

The Kuskokwim River, Vol. 15, No. 4. $19.95.

Katmai Country, Vol. 16, No. 1. $19.95.

North Slope Now, Vol. 16, No. 2. $19.95.

The Tanana Basin, Vol. 16, No. 3. $19.95.

The Copper Trail, Vol. 16, No. 4. $19.95.

The Nushagak Basin, Vol. 17, No. 1. $19.95.

Juneau, Vol. 17, No. 2. Out of print.

The Middle Yukon River, Vol. 17, No. 3. $19.95.

The Lower Yukon River, Vol. 17, No. 4. $19.95.

Alaska's Weather, Vol. 18, No. 1. $19.95.

Alaska's Volcanoes, Vol. 18, No. 2. $19.95.

Admiralty Island: Fortress of Bears, Vol. 18, No. 3. $19.95.

Unalaska/Dutch Harbor, Vol. 18, No. 4. $19.95.

Skagway: A Legacy of Gold, Vol. 19, No. 1. $19.95.

ALASKA: The Great Land, Vol. 19, No. 2. $19.95.

Kodiak, Vol. 19, No. 3. $19.95.

Alaska's Railroads, Vol. 19, No. 4. $19.95.

Prince William Sound, Vol. 20, No. 1. $19.95.

Southeast Alaska, Vol. 20, No. 2. $19.95.

Arctic National Wildlife Refuge, Vol. 20, No. 3. $19.95.

Alaska's Bears, Vol. 20, No. 4. $19.95.

The Alaska Peninsula, Vol. 21, No. 1. $19.95.

The Kenai Peninsula, Vol. 21, No. 2. $19.95.

People of Alaska, Vol. 21, No. 3. $19.95.

Prehistoric Alaska, Vol. 21, No. 4. $19.95.

Fairbanks, Vol. 22, No. 1. $19.95.

The Aleutian Islands, Vol. 22, No. 2. $19.95.

Rich Earth: Alaska's Mineral Industry, Vol. 22, No. 3. $19.95.

World War II in Alaska, Vol. 22, No. 4. $19.95.

Anchorage, Vol. 23, No. 1. $21.95.

Native Cultures in Alaska, Vol. 23, No. 2. $19.95.

The Brooks Range, Vol. 23, No. 3. $19.95.

Moose, Caribou and Muskox, Vol. 23, No. 4. $19.95.

Alaska's Southern Panhandle, Vol. 24, No. 1. $19.95.

PRICES AND AVAILABILITY SUBJECT TO CHANGE

Membership in The Alaska Geographic Society includes a subscription to *ALASKA GEOGRAPHIC*®, the Society's colorful, award-winning quarterly.

Call or write for current membership rates or to request a free catalog. *ALASKA GEOGRAPHIC*® back issues are also available (see above list). **NOTE:** This list was current in mid-1997. If more than a year or two have elapsed since that time, please contact us before ordering to check prices and availability of specific back issues.

When ordering back issues please add $2 postage/handling per book for Book Rate; $4 each for Priority Mail. Inquire for non-U.S. postage rates. To order, send check or money order (U.S. funds) or VISA/MasterCard information (including expiration date and your phone number) with list of titles desired to:

ALASKA GEOGRAPHIC.

P.O. Box 93370 • Anchorage, AK 99509-3370
Phone: (907) 562-0164 • Fax (907) 562-0479

NEXT ISSUE:

COMMERCIAL FISHING IN ALASKA

Vol. 24, No. 3. One of the three most important industries in Alaska, commercial fishing runs the gamut from high-value crab and salmon to high-volume fisheries like pollock. This issue reviews the entire industry in the words and insights of a former commercial fishermen. To members, fall 1997. $19.95.